COMPOUNDED FAITH

PEGGY LAKIN

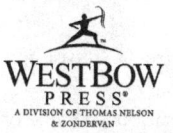

WestBow
PRESS®
A DIVISION OF THOMAS NELSON
& ZONDERVAN

Copyright © 2021 Peggy Lakin.

All rights reserved. No part of this book may be used or reproduced by any means, graphic, electronic, or mechanical, including photocopying, recording, taping or by any information storage retrieval system without the written permission of the author except in the case of brief quotations embodied in critical articles and reviews.

This book is a work of non-fiction. Unless otherwise noted, the author and the publisher make no explicit guarantees as to the accuracy of the information contained in this book and in some cases, names of people and places have been altered to protect their privacy.

WestBow Press books may be ordered through booksellers or by contacting:

WestBow Press
A Division of Thomas Nelson & Zondervan
1663 Liberty Drive
Bloomington, IN 47403
www.westbowpress.com
844-714-3454

Because of the dynamic nature of the Internet, any web addresses or links contained in this book may have changed since publication and may no longer be valid. The views expressed in this work are solely those of the author and do not necessarily reflect the views of the publisher, and the publisher hereby disclaims any responsibility for them.

Any people depicted in stock imagery provided by Getty Images are models, and such images are being used for illustrative purposes only. Certain stock imagery © Getty Images.

Scripture quotations taken from The Holy Bible, New International Version® NIV® Copyright © 1973 1978 1984 2011 by Biblica, Inc. TM. Used by permission. All rights reserved worldwide.

ISBN: 978-1-6642-1963-2 (sc)
ISBN: 978-1-6642-1962-5 (hc)
ISBN: 978-1-6642-1964-9 (e)

Library of Congress Control Number: 2021901513

Print information available on the last page.

WestBow Press rev. date: 01/29/2021

CHAPTER 1

Joe Lakin and I were high school sweethearts; we accomplished a lot and failed at so much in our time together. The more that time moves on, the more I realize how much God has had His hands on us and would continue to move through us and with us.

Joe was born in 1950, and I was born in 1952. Each of us was born into a family that was broken, in different ways. His father left their family soon after the sixth child was born. Both my parents were alcoholics; I had two older sisters when our parents divorced. My father remarried, and I had a stepmother and three more sisters: a house full of six girls.

Joe grew up in a small town, where everybody knew everybody and watched out for each other. He was fortunate to be able to live in that same town all his life and attended the same Catholic church.

I, on the other hand, was not that fortunate. When my mother and father were still married, we moved around more times than I could count. After the divorce, my father received custody of my two sisters and me; we seemed to move around a lot too. I was in a different school almost every year until I started high school, and then, I actually was able to go to the same school for four years. I was so excited to get to do that; it really meant a lot to me. I know that may sound silly, but it was important to me; it was something I had not been able to do.

Joe and I met in high school; he was a year ahead of me. He asked me out a few times, but I always said no for some reason or another. The truth was that I couldn't date until I was sixteen, but I didn't want him to know because it was almost my birthday. I thought if he found out, he'd never ask me out again. As it happened, one evening when he was at our house, my younger sister told Joe I couldn't go out with him because I couldn't date yet. I was really upset and thought, *Oh, no; this is it. He's never going to ask me out again.* But he did, and I was so thankful, because I liked him a lot.

During my high school years, I would go to school in the morning and work in the school office in the afternoon. I babysat in the evening, when I wasn't at home cooking or cleaning the house. You see, Dad was gone through the week because he was an over-the-road truck driver; Wilma, my stepmom, worked in the evenings as a cook. We three older girls took care of things at home, watching the three younger girls while Mom and Dad were working. I would get up before five every morning and would waitress at a small café; I also shucked corn in the summer months.

After Joe graduated from high school, he decided to go to beauty school and become a hairdresser; I continued to work. Joe and I were married in 1971, before we had a home of our own. I had an apartment, but with Joe going to school, it was hard for us to make it, so we moved into his mom's small house. We lived there for a while, but after Joe got out of beauty school and got a job, we moved into our own apartment. We continued to work hard and decided to have a family. We had two sons, Tony and Brian. They've grown up to be hard-working, family-oriented men involved in their church; worshipping God is a priority to them.

Joe and I continued to work hard. Joe was a hairdresser during the day, and I worked part-time so I could be home with the boys. One day, Joe received a call to see if he was interested in tearing down a house. That one house led to many other house demolitions over the next several years. We both loved tearing down an old house piece by piece to make something look better. We also restored several homes while we were living in them. The man we rented from told us he would reduce our rent if we did some restorations to the house, so we did. As we look back now, we realize that God had His hand on us, step by step and board by board, to get us where we are today. You see, we built a large two-story home out of used lumber. We built the home ourselves and with help from several friends. After we lived there several years, we really felt God speaking to us about being debt free, so we sold that house and bought the home we are living in now, paying cash for it.

But guess what? This home was built in 1903, and it needed to be restored. I was so excited to restore this house. I remember the day we looked at it. It had so much character; I loved it. But as Joe and the Realtor were looking at things outside, our son Tony and I were looking things over inside. I remember Tony and I talked about how this house would work if we could move this wall, move the stairway, put a wall right here and another wall over here; the list went on and on. When Joe came back in, I told him that I loved the house, but we would have to make some changes. Imagine that. He smiled and rolled his eyes at the same time. I'd seen that look before, but it was a good look. It says, "Are you sure?" Like I said, there was just something that we enjoyed about tearing things apart and making it better. So here we go; doing a little at a time, as money would allow.

I think it was the idea of restoring something old and making it into something new; this transformation was so exciting to me. We could apply this technique to something material or to our daily walk in life. Several years ago, when Joe and I would go to auctions, I often found an old piece of furniture that I thought I needed to restore. I couldn't wait to use a furniture stripper on it, clean it, and then refinish it. It was so exciting to see the completed product. Then, of course, it was fun to tell the story about getting it from the old look to the new. As we continued to walk through life, we tore down several old houses in town and were able to see contractors build new homes where the old one used to sit. I had no idea that all this hard work was to teach us the principle of never giving up. In order to restore something, we had to be very patient, diligent, and calm; we had a vision and never let go of it. We hoped this would help us get to where we needed to be in God's plan for our lives.

While we were restoring our house, Joe came down with contact dermatitis on his hands, and that's not good for a hairdresser. He had to close his shop and find another job. Unfortunately, during that time, I had already quit my job. It was a really hard time for Joe and me, and we wondered how we were going to eat and pay the utilities. The boys still lived at home, but they both worked and helped us when they could. It was a dark time for us, though. We kept wondering where God was because we kept praying, but nothing would happen (that we could see). Life just kept getting harder, and we became more frustrated, to the point where Joe didn't want to go to church, so I went by myself. He had reached the point of accepting that this was just the way our lives were going to be. Life had always been hard, and it wasn't going to change.

Joe found a job working with a recruiter, but that didn't last long, and he went to work for a company spraying chemicals. He was not as happy as when he was a hairdresser, though. Joe just thrived being around people, and what better place to do that than doing people's hair?

It just so happened that Jack, one of Joe's buddies, offered Joe a place to put his hair shop; he didn't even charge him anything. Talk about an answer to prayer. It was perfect for Joe, and he was able to do hair again because the dermatitis on his hands had healed.

I, on the other hand, could not find a job anywhere, so I decided to try my hand at cleaning houses. I was able to do as many houses as I wanted, so before long, I was cleaning thirteen houses. Around the same time, I saw in the paper that the dental school in Alton was hiring. I thought I might as well try for it. My sister Susie spoke to me about the position; she knew someone who worked there, so she gave me her name and phone number. I called her, and she told me about the test for the position and said she would help me any way she could. I took the test and was given an interview. I had an interview, and Susie's friend put in a good word for me, but it was not going to work for me. The hours of the job were from one in the afternoon until ten o'clock in the evening. I was disappointed because I knew I couldn't drive home that late at night.

Then guess what happened? Three days later, I was called about an interview for another position, in the school's business office. This interview was for a daytime position. I was excited and knew that this was from God. This notice came to me exactly three days after I decided not to take the first position, which I had been offered. Then, three days after I interviewed for the second position, I was offered that job and accepted. I started my job in October of 1998.

I don't dream very often, and when I do, I don't remember all of it; maybe pieces of it, but not enough of it to put it all together. There was one dream I had in the middle of summer in 1998 that I'll never forget. As I type this, I can sense the feelings that always come back when I talk about it. I was sitting at a very large table in the dark. I was by myself, and it was so dark, it was black. I couldn't even see my hand in front of my face. I heard a noise like someone was in the house, and it startled me, but I continued to sit at the table. I heard the noise again, and it was so loud that I jumped up.

I yelled, "Who is it, who's there?"

I entered the room, but it was so dark that I couldn't see anything or anyone. I moved around until I found a light switch; I tried and tried and tried to get the light to come on, but it wouldn't turn on. I was getting so upset that the light would not come on, but I kept trying and trying. I knew that I had turned that light on before, but it wouldn't come on for me. Just then, someone walked in front of me, but I wasn't afraid. I reached out and touched the person's shoulder. It was soft and warm.

Just then, the person took my hand, kissed the back of my hand, and said, "It is Christ."

I tried to speak but couldn't. I will never forget that voice and still remember the softness and warmth of His shoulder, but I never saw His face. As God's Word says, "You cannot see the face of God and live." My body was shaking and trembling, just from being in the awesome presence of Jesus. Just then, my eyes flew open, and I sat up in the bed and looked around to see Jesus because I knew He was there. I was still shaking, and my body was drenched with sweat.

I woke Joe up and said, "Joe, Joe, Jesus is here. He's here, Joe."

He looked around but didn't see anyone. I was still shaking, so Joe held me to try to calm me down. I was crying and still looking around the room because His presence was so real. I couldn't close my eyes because Jesus had been here. He kissed the back of my hand. John 1:5 says, "The light shines in the darkness, but the darkness has not understood it."

I, of course, could not go back to sleep but wondered what this dream could mean. It was the first time in a long time that I had a dream and remembered all of it. Darkness so thick that I couldn't see anything, but Jesus let me know that He was with me. I for sure could not think straight and could not quit crying, so the next morning, I called Toni, a friend of mine, and told her the dream. She cried too and then told me that I had been in darkness for a long time and couldn't see any light. At times, I wondered if there was light at the end of the tunnel. I could not get the light to come on with my own power, and I could not see the light in the darkness, but Jesus is the light.

Christ wanted to tell me that he has always been in the darkness with me, in all the dark times we had gone through and in the darkness to come. As far as my body being wet, in scripture, there is a washing by the Word and a cleansing that comes. When something so awesome happens, then our natural tendencies kick in. Little did I know that I would soon be in darkness like I had never seen before. Be courageous, fear not; I've always wanted to be in God's will. This must be it. Would God give us something before we are ready? Jesus showed me that He would be the light in the darkness. Isaiah 42:16 says, "I will lead the blind by ways they have not known, along unfamiliar paths I will guide them: I will turn the darkness into light before them and make the rough places smooth. These are the things I will do: I will not forsake them."

CHAPTER 2

Day star shine down on me. Let your
love shine through me in the night.

Lead me Lord I'll follow, anywhere
you open up the door.

Let your word speak to me, show me
what I've never seen before.

Lord I want to be your witness. You can
take what's wrong and make it right.

Day star shine down on me. Let your
love shine through me in the night.

I want to tell you how the words to this song became very real for me. I didn't know, but these words would become a part of my life one day; they helped me make it through each day. I needed God to shine down on me, especially when I went through dark times. I said that if He continued to lead me, I would follow Him, but I needed the wisdom that comes only from Him. I said, "Lord, I know You can take what's wrong and make it right; I need You to do this, another time. I want to be Your witness. So God, please shine down on me and bring your love to me, even in the dark times."

It's easier to find God in the good times, but He's hard to find when things seem to be going wrong. There were so many days and nights that I needed God to be standing near me.

As I was walking one day, I was talking to God and asking Him to be with me and thanking Him for directing my steps. I was talking to Him about this story, and I told Him that I didn't know how to write a book, but I knew that He did. After all, He gave the writers of the Bible the words to put on paper, and the Bible is still touching lives today. That's what I want this story to do: touch somebody's life.

It's been thirteen years since I first thought about writing this story. There continued to be this still small voice inside me that kept saying to write it down, and God even sent people my way to confirm His voice. I kept talking myself out of starting this story until now.

I recently heard a pastor preach about the "whisper of God." The whisper of God? That must have been it. I heard a soft voice telling me to write this story, but it was so many years ago. I heard the pastor say that if we told God, "Here I am," and obeyed, then great would be your reward. The reward? That people would have a personal relationship with God because of this story.

In Matthew 10:19–20, Jesus was speaking to the disciples; He told them, "Do not worry about what to say or how to say it. At that time, you will be given what to say for it will not be you speaking but the Spirit of your father speaking through you."

As I look back, I still don't know why the accident happened. I call it an accident but that's not quite the correct word to use, since everything happens for a reason. Everything is timely. God is in control and is to be glorified in all things. So many lives were touched and so many miracles happened through the accident. I feel like now is the time for this story; God recently sent a man to our house, who encouraged me to put this story on paper. I had never met this man before; he came to see our house, which belonged to his great-grandfather years ago. He did not even know that I had been thinking of writing this story. As we showed him the house, we did a lot of talking about restoring the house and that led to Joe's accident.

I told a friend of mine about this man, and she told me, "Get started, and don't quit. Don't give up, and don't let the devil steal this away from you." She said he tried to steal it from me in the past, but I should tell my story from my heart because that's where the story is.

Another friend of mine said that I had to do this. She told me several years ago that I needed to put the story on paper. I know a lot of people have had great experiences with God and have been touched by Him in a special way; some had out-of-body experiences, and others were even healed by the Lord. So what would make this story different? I'll let you decide as you read through the pages. I've been told that no matter what happened in my life, I never gave up, so I didn't want to give up on this book, either.

March 1, 1999, began like any other day. It was a Monday, so Joe's hair shop was closed. Since he worked on Saturdays, Sunday and Monday were his days off, sort of. When Joe wasn't working in the shop, he was working at some other job. It was not unusual for him to be asked if he would like to do some job or another, even if he would never done it before. He really loved doing things for other people. It didn't matter who it was; he was ready to go.

On this Monday, I was going to go to work, and Joe was going out to do some work at my mom and dad's house. A storm had passed through Berdan, the small community where my parents lived, back in the fall, and it had damaged several trees. My dad had been diagnosed with cancer and was unable to take care of the trees, so he had mentioned that the trees needed to be cleaned up. Of course, Joe said that he'd take care of that job when the weather was good. This was the day.

I was getting ready for work, and Joe left to go to Jerseyville and get a lift so he could trim the tree limbs that needed it. I left for work and saw Joe on his way back; we waved at each other and gave each other a big smile. He knew I would be smiling, and I knew he would be because we loved seeing each other. I really didn't want him to do the tree trimming, but he was used to doing odd jobs.

The day went on as usual; I finished work at 5:30 p.m. It was the time of year that it was beginning to get dark earlier, so it was dark when I got home about forty minutes later. The boys were home, but Joe wasn't; I figured he was still visiting with Mom because he loved to talk. I went into the house and began to change into some comfy clothes for the evening, when I heard a voice yelling from the back door.

It was my mom's voice, yelling, "Joe's been hurt, and they took him to the hospital." I came running to the back door, and she said, "You better get down there."

My first thought was that Joe had been hurt while working jobs before and it never was bad, so I hoped this wasn't bad, either. I yelled to the boys, and we left for the hospital; when we got there, the waiting room was full of people who already knew that Joe had been injured.

I opened the door of the emergency room, and Joe was lying on a bed, holding a cold pack on his head. His head was bandaged, so I really couldn't see anything. Joe's sister was with him, and she just looked at me and shook her head from side to side.

Joe looked up, and when he saw me, he said, "Hi, Bunk. I'm going to be fine. A tree limb hit me in the head."

I stayed with him for a few minutes; I was trying to be strong but felt sick to my stomach. I went out and told the boys that Joe was awake and talking, but we didn't know how bad the injury was. Yet.

I began to ask around to see if anyone knew what happened. I found out that he was working on the last tree that needed to be trimmed. He was in the lift when the chainsaw got jammed in the limb. He went down to get a rope to help release the saw. He got back up to the limb, and as he tried to get the saw out of the limb, the branch snapped and hit Joe in the front of his head.

He was able to use the controls on the lift to lower himself to the ground. He somehow walked over to my mom's back porch and sat down on the steps; he told Mom that he would get back up there as soon as his head stopped spinning.

Mom then told him he wasn't going back up there and the ambulance was on the way; he did not know how badly he was hurt.

I was told that the ambulance got to Mom's in record time.

Everyone on the crew knew Joe. One of the crew asked him questions to make sure he was still coherent. She asked him his name, address, phone number, the year, and the president of the United States. I found out later that Joe had made a comical comment to her on the way to the hospital. He answered all the questions correctly, which was amazing. I learned later that there was no way that Joe could have got himself down from the tree, let alone walk over to the back porch. He should not have been able to have a discussion with Mom or with the ambulance crew. The limb had damaged the frontal lobe of his skull, and gray matter was protruding from his forehead. God was already there.

I was also told that the hospital officials weren't reporting the accident to the public because they didn't have room for all the people who would come. Everyone loved Joe.

Joe's condition began to change rapidly. His body started to respond to what had happened. The doctor came out and took the boys and me into a small room to tell us what they were doing.

After a while, he became unresponsive. The doctor suggested that we pray. After the doctor left the room, through all our tears, we tried to pray.

They took Joe to another room to insert a breathing tube. I was standing in the hall outside the room and could hear the nurses and the doctor yelling Joe's name, over and over, telling him to wake up. I felt faint and fell to the floor. I thought that they were losing him. I could hear this for quite some time, and the doctor came out and said they were having difficulty intubating him; Joe was fighting them, moving and kicking around a lot, and he bit the hand of one of the other doctors. By this time, people started filling the halls, because they heard what had happened.

While all of this was going on, I learned that Joe had to be moved to another hospital. By this time, he was in critical condition. They asked where I wanted Joe to be taken. It was so difficult to think clearly, and I really didn't have time to think much about what our insurance would do. In the past, Joe and I never had insurance; we couldn't afford it. I got insurance after I started working at the dental school in October of 1998; Joe's head injury was on March 1, 1999. The works of God are so timely.

We learned that they would be bringing in a helicopter so they could take him to the next hospital faster. Before I knew it, the helicopter was there; we were told that Joe would be brought out on a stretcher. His head was totally bandaged. They had determined that he had severe inner cranial pressure.

We were in the hall waiting for him to come out on the stretcher, and Joe's mom was standing next to me; when she saw him, she almost fell to the floor. It was a shock for everyone there to see Joe in this kind of state. Someone who was so vibrant and full of life could not even breathe on his own. I leaned over and whispered that I loved him and said the boys and I would be on our way.

It took us an hour to get to where he was being flown; I couldn't go with him in the helicopter. As he was taken out of the hospital, the boys grabbed me, and we went out to our car. I had tears in my eyes and kept trying to look at Joe, but the boys told me not to look over at the helicopter. I knew it was bad and didn't know if he'd be alive when we got to Springfield.

CHAPTER 3

The trip to Springfield took forever. All I could do was cry; I tried to pray, but it was hard to do because I was so upset. I know I was in a state of shock. I kept going over the events of the evening in my mind and wondered how and why this was happening. Joe and I were so happy. We didn't have much, each other, two great boys, and we were crazy about each other.

We finally arrived at the hospital in Springfield, and when we went into the emergency room, a nurse grabbed my hand and rushed me to the surgical area. There was no time to waste; the surgeon was waiting for me to get there to sign papers to okay the surgery. I wish I could have ridden in the helicopter, because I would have already been there, and the surgery could have been started sooner. My prayers were answered, though, because God took care of Joe until I got there to sign the papers.

The nurse then took me into a waiting room; the surgeon came out and told me that Joe's condition was extremely critical. He said that he would do what he could, but he didn't know if Joe would make it through the surgery. I asked God what to do, because Joe had told me time and time again that he did not want to be kept alive by a machine because he would be ready to be with Jesus.

However, I kept hearing a small voice telling me to sign the papers, so I did. I was then taken to a larger waiting room, filled with about fifty people. I just sat down in a chair and cried. After a while, the surgeon came out and told us he had removed blood clots, leaves, and tree bark from Joe's brain. He then said that he could not do this on his own but would need God to direct his hands. He said this was the worst head injury he had ever seen, and he had seen a lot. He previously worked in a trauma center. I knew that we were where we were supposed to be.

I then asked everybody in the waiting room to sing praise and worship songs. My sister Rae and I walked back and forth in the hallway, and I could just feel that the worship was traveling into the operating room. I just knew that it would, and that God would be there, because He will dwell in the praises of His people, and we are called by God to worship Him. *Worship* means to adore, exalt, love, lift our voices, and bow down before Him. So that is what we did.

After a short time, the chaplain came in to see how we were doing. She asked us to all stand in a circle, hold hands, and pray. Everyone in the room got in a circle and began to pray. This lasted for several minutes, and the anointing was clearly present. When I opened my eyes, I saw many people sending prayers up to heaven for Joe. I knew again that we were where we were supposed to be. The surgeon and nurse continued to come out and give us reports on how the surgery was going. He kept telling us he still wasn't sure that Joe was going to make it.

At one point, after talking to us, he said, "You keep doing what you are doing in here, and I'll keep doing what I do in there."

The praise must have been reaching the surgery room. We waited and waited, and we praised and praised. I remember sitting in that room, looking at those who came to be with us, and crying. By this time, it was the wee hours of the morning. Micah 7:7 says, "But as for me I watch in hope for the Lord. I wait for God my Savior; my God will hear me." So I had a choice to make. Was I going to totally fall apart, or was I going to trust God?

The surgery lasted three hours, and then Joe was moved into ICU. The chaplain took me and the boys to an elevator reserved for family members of patients who've had surgery. We were taken to a small waiting room, while the doctor and nurses got Joe situated in

ICU. It seemed like forever before we were told we could see him. He had a compound fracture of the skull, multiple facial fractures, a broken upper jaw that moved in and out, and fractured ribs.

A nurse took us back to see Joe, but the boys just couldn't go in. Brian had been physically sick for several hours, and Tony was just not ready to see his dad. It was just too hard for him. I was told not to talk, but to be perfectly quiet; the pressure on his inner cranium was so high that he couldn't be disturbed. I could not believe what I was seeing. It was Joe, but it didn't look like him. He was connected to so many machines that I couldn't count all of them. I leaned over to look at him; his face swollen and badly bruised.

He had sterile wraps around his head and was connected to a breathing machine (breathing on his own would have been too much for his body). A tube came out of the top of his head to monitor the inner cranial pressure; it was 30 to 40, and normal was 10. The cranial pressure, blood pressure, and oxygen levels were alarmingly high. A drain tube was inserted in Joe's right lung because his fractured ribs caused fluid to build up.

His face and head were very swollen, and his mouth, tongue, eyes, and ears were purple because of bruising. His temperature kept spiking, so the nurses put a cooling blanket over and under him. It was so difficult to see Joe lying there, so lifeless, and just then, he moved his toes and fingers. The surgeon said that there was no way humanly possible that he should have been able to do anything like that.

The surgeon then told me that after looking at Joe's medical chart, he was very surprised he was still alive; it was a miracle. I still could not speak to him or touch him, but from the time the surgeon told me that Joe had received a miracle, I once again knew that God was with us. Joe and I had done everything together, and we would do this too, with God's help. I couldn't help but be reminded of Isaiah 42:16: "I will lead the blind by ways they have not known, along unfamiliar paths I will guide them and make the rough places smooth. These are the things I will do. I will not forsake them."

The waiting room was full of people, waiting to hear about Joe. I would go in and check on him and then come back to give a report.

I knew that I was still in shock. This still did not seem real to me; things like this just didn't happen to us, but God does have a purpose for each of us. I would not have chosen to go down this road, but I love God and knew that He would never leave me alone. God's Word says that He will never fail the people who put their trust in Him. I knew there was a huge battle to fight, but Psalm 55:16–18 says, "But I call to God and the Lord saves me, evening, morning and noon. I cry out in distress and he hears my voice. He ransoms me unharmed from the battle waged against me, even though many oppose me."

I have felt for years that I truly loved and trusted God, but after I went down this path, I found out there is a whole new level of faith when you depend on Him totally. There have been so many times that only God could have moved us through a situation, something we could not have done on our own. Sometimes, I felt like it was not really me going through this, but someone totally different. 2 Corinthians 10: 4–5 says, "The weapons we fight with are not the weapons for the world. On the contrary, they have divine power to demolish strongholds. We demolish arguments and every pretension that sets itself up against the knowledge of God and we take captive every thought to make it obedient to Christ."

The days and nights began to run into each other, and I had no idea what time it was. I don't remember when I ate last. People kept coming to the hospital to check on Joe, and there were so many phone calls that I couldn't talk to everyone. Other family members and friends helped take some of the calls for me. There were so many people in the halls who came to see us, but I didn't get to speak to all of them. As I was looking down the hall, I saw Paul. He was like one of our own kids because he spent so much time at our house as he and our boys were growing up. I had to go to him and give him a huge hug. The love and support for our family, from friends and hometown people, and from people we didn't even know, was truly amazing. I was told that the prayers had even gone global; some people overseas were praying for Joe. What a blessing it was when Bill, our friend who lives in another state, made sure we had lots of minutes on a phone card, because so many calls needed to be made.

Some people who came to the hospital spent the night and prayed in the chapel. This went on night after night. One evening, two brothers, John and Rich, came over to pray; when they saw me, they said they had not planned to come to the hospital, but something seemed to be drawing them up there, and it could not be ignored, so they stayed and prayed through the night.

Just before a group of us went to the chapel, Joe's temperature spiked to 104 degrees; they put a cooling blanket under him, but we knew that only God could bring the temperature down. I tried to keep my mind off what I thought humans could do for Joe and think about what God was doing for him.

I need to tell you about a letter or prayer that Joe received from Ben, the eleven-year-old son of our dear friends. This is what Ben prayed for Joe:

Dear Jesus,

We're here to talk to You about Joe Lakin. He's so special to me, Father. I thank You now because I know You are going to take care of him.

Satan, I know I'm not very big, but in the Name of Jesus and by the power of His Blood, I come against you for Joe Lakin! In Jesus's Name, I claim healing for Joe, complete healing. Yes, there will be a scar or two, that's going to be Joe's tool to use against you, Satan, to tell all the people, "Look at what Satan tried to do to me. But see what God has done." Thank You, God, that Joe will tell thousands of people of Your miracles in his life, and many, many lives will change.

Thank You Lord, in Jesus's Name,

Amen

Ben, such a young boy, prayed for Joe in such a special and big way. I'll never forget how that prayer made me feel, and as I read it again, I get those same feelings. Because I know Ben so well, I know that it truly came from his heart.

After chapel, the boys and I went back to Joe's room, but on the way, we saw two young girls walking by, and they were crying uncontrollably. Their dad had been in ICU for several days but had taken a turn for the worse. We stayed with them and prayed for them that God would give them strength to make it through this hard time. Unfortunately, their dad did pass away later that night, but they came and thanked us for being there for them. It was great to be able to be used by God, even when we are going through such a difficult time.

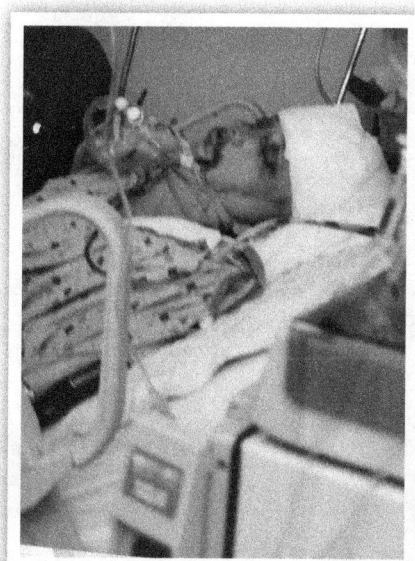 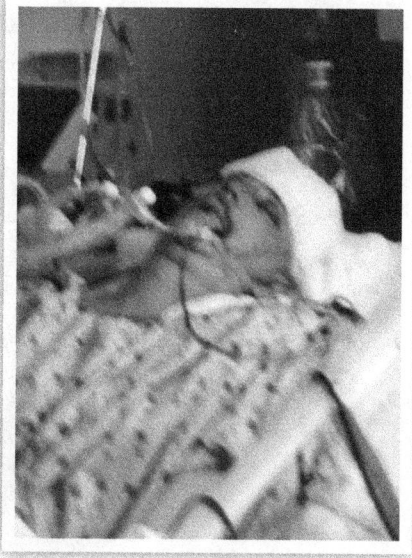

N.S. (cont)
O: S/p op c̄ general surgery this AM - pt may need chest tube on (R).
A: S/p crani for multiple skull fx, evac. of epidural hematoma - Stable at this time
P: Will consult Dr Henkle for vent management. Cont current orders. Monitor neuro status closely.

IT is Remarkable + A MIRACLE That is "AWAKE" follows commands -
One Henovac int   M x Kelley - Emergency Dr.
     Post-op CT shows contusions are worse but ICP better - no mannitol needed.
Still in critical condition -

CHAPTER 4

The accident happened on a Monday, and on Saturday, they took Joe for a CT scan; Tony saw him as he was being pushed down the hallway, and it was terribly hard for him to see his father that way. The CT showed there was still extreme swelling on his brain, but no extra bleeding, so that was great news. By this time, several people had called to tell me they had been praying for Joe; they couldn't sleep at night. God kept waking them up, and they knew it was time to pray for Joe. Some of them had dreams showing them that Joe was going to be just fine.

On Saturday, the surgeon suggested we try to wake Joe up. He wanted us to get Joe to respond more. I talked to Joe so loudly that I strained my vocal cords, but I didn't care if it would wake him up. This was not about me, but about God and about Joe. His blood pressure was being watched closely, and his inner cranial pressure was still up and down; it got as high as 32. They kept trying to get his body to accept the feeding tube in his upper shoulder, but it was still not working for him. A friend of ours, who was also a doctor, came to see Joe and told me that after reading his chart, he really did not think he was going to make it; he suggested I prepare myself, but I did not accept that. Psalm 28:7 states that "the Lord is my strength and my shield, my heart trusts in Him and I am helped."

I had to keep believing that God was not going to let go of Joe. When I thought about how much he loves the Lord, I mean really, deep down loves the Lord, I recalled Psalm 18, which says, "He reached down from on high and took hold of me; He drew me out of deep waters. He rescued me from my powerful enemy, from my foes, who were too strong for me. They confronted me in the day of my disaster, but the Lord was my support. He brought me out into a spacious place; he rescued me because he delighted in me."

It made me believe that God regarded Joe as a friend; He saved him. That was what I would hang onto.

I had learned quickly to elevate and rely on my faith. So many things were going on with Joe that I couldn't do anything but put my trust in God to make it through, just one day. As I was reading God's Word, I found in Psalm 56, which says, "When I am afraid, I will trust in You. In God's word I praise, in God I will trust, I will not be afraid."

The fifth day that Joe was in ICU, two ladies from our hometown came to see how we were doing. One of them had tears in her eyes and told me she needed to see Joe. Her voice sounded desperate. She just kept saying that she needed to see Joe. I had to ask and make sure that it was okay with the doctor for me to take someone in who wasn't family. To my surprise, they said it was okay, so I took them in to see him. This woman bent down next to Joe's ear and said that she needed him to wake up and tell her again how much she needs the Lord in her life and that the Lord loves her.

I was standing at the foot of his bed and didn't know if he could hear me, but I said to him, "Joe, cry out to the power of God that is inside of you, and summon the Holy Spirit to help you, and somehow give her a sign to let her know that God loves her."

Just then, both of Joe's hands and feet moved at the same time. We were all crying. When I told the doctor what Joe did, he said there was no way that could have happened, not all at one time. Joe's mind was not working to be able to do that, but God was with us.

A little later in the evening, I was in his room with Toni, a friend of mine, and Joe's inner cranial pressure spiked extremely high; the nurse told us not to talk to him for a bit, to see if we were stimulating him or if it was the pain. We left to go to the chapel to pray and saw our friend Jack, who was already there praying. I walked around, praying, and suddenly started laughing uncontrollably; Toni started laughing too. Then the Holy Spirit also fell on Jack, and he laughed so hard that he fell on the floor. The anointing was all over us; we could feel the Spirit of God with us. I needed that kind of assurance with me. We did not realize that there were cameras in the chapel, and a couple of security guards came in to make sure that we were all okay. We, of course, said that we were (not wanting to tell them that we were under the influence; they would not have understood).

Several of us decided to get together to have a praise and worship service in the chapel. It was a special time; Toni brought her keyboard so we would have music. I cried through most of it, but at the same time, I recalled so many things that God had done for Joe. The Lord spoke to me and told me that Joe was in the palm of His hand; He was telling him supernatural things that needed to be told in the natural. I pondered this thought and kept it close to my heart. The next day, two different people called and told me that they had a dream the night before, and a third person told me that God told her that He was telling Joe supernatural things. When I spoke to JL on the phone, he told me that Joe was being told secret things by God. He also told me that he felt like it was an honor to have been able to see Joe. I was so excited and touched because these people confirmed what God had told me.

We were excited later that day because the doctor removed the machine that was monitoring his inner cranial pressure; they also took the bandages off, and Joe was breathing more on his own. When the surgeon came in, he told me that Joe had made great progress over the weekend. He said that he didn't know if or when Joe would ever wake up; it could be this week, next week, or months away, if ever. I felt like he was saying, "With this man, who knows?" Joe had come so far, so fast.

Joe's dad came to see him that day, for the first time since the accident. He was with Joe when the accident happened, and he could not get the picture of Joe getting hurt out of his mind. He just needed to see Joe for himself and to make sure that he was okay.

On March 7, we learned that Joe was going to be moved to Memorial Hospital, just a few blocks away. The hospital we had been at was not covered by my insurance, but since it was an emergency, the insurance covered everything. Memorial was on my insurance plan, so they took him there next. It was really hard to leave the doctors and nurses we had grown so close to. It felt like we were leaving family.

The night Joe was moved, it was snowing hard, and the snow was so deep that I wasn't sure we'd make it even a few blocks. It was very late by the time we got to Memorial, and it took a long time to get Joe situated in ICU. A nurse came out to get me when it was okay to see him. My friend Toni and I went in, and the nurse began to tell me things about Joe. His blood pressure was good after the move, and he was breathing on his own, which was very good.

Then she began to tell me that Joe would not be the same person. She said that he would not walk or talk the same, and his personality would be different. She wanted to know if anyone had told me that, and I told her that they had not. Because of the severity of the injury, and where it was located on the left side of the brain, everything would change.

I couldn't believe what I was hearing. I was expecting Joe to be Joe.

I almost fell to the floor, but Toni grabbed hold of me and whispered in my ear, "Whose report will we believe? We will believe the report of the Lord."

The next day, when I was sitting next to Joe, he yawned for the first time and moved his head from side to side; I was truly surprised. The nurse asked us to bring tennis shoes for him to wear and to hang family pictures in the room. We could play music in his room too, so we found a Christian station on the radio. I thought that when Joe did wake up, he would be upset with me for putting him through all of this. Everyone kept telling me that I didn't have a choice, saying that Joe never did leave us, and he wasn't being kept alive by a machine. I just wanted God to breathe into this situation again, and I knew that "not by might, nor by power, but by my Spirit, says the Lord."

Later that afternoon, I received a phone call that a group of young people from Pensacola, Florida, were coming to the hospital to pray for Joe. That was so exciting, but I wasn't sure if the nurse would let so many people in Joe's room at one time. I had to ask the head nurse, and when I told her about them, she got excited too. She was familiar with the Pensacola Revival and wanted to be in Joe's room to pray with the group when they came. She told me that she couldn't wait.

After they arrived, we all walked into Joe's room, closed the door, and began to pray, in one accord. God's glory filled the room. After we prayed, we went to the chapel, and everyone gathered around me and the boys and laid hands on us and began to pray. Then, one of the young men in the group wanted to play the organ so we could sing praise and worship. He couldn't find the switch to turn it on, so I said I would find the chaplain to see if it we could play the organ. Just as I stepped out of the chapel, I heard the organ.

I went to find the chaplain. I found his office and knocked on the door, but there was no answer. When I got back to the chapel, I could see people with hands raised, singing beautiful worship to the sounds of the organ. I joined in, and after a few minutes, I heard someone walk in. I turned to look, and it was the chaplain. He joined in worship with hands raised and singing with everything he had. We continued for quite a while, and when we were done, we all went over to the chaplain and laid hands on him and began to pray for him.

He was so excited that we were all there and kept saying, "Praise the Lord," again and again. He then said, "I cannot tell you how long it's been since that organ has been played. I have never heard worship like this in this chapel."

He asked us where we were all from, and it was so funny, because we were all from somewhere different. He hated to see us leave but said that he would continue to lift up Joe and me and the boys in prayer. This was a very long day and night, and I still couldn't remember when I slept last.

The next day, we began to play worship music in Joe's room, and the nurses told us that his blood pressure and other numbers went up; they would have to sedate him. They were not sure if the music caused him to be restless, or if it was pain. I was wondering if being unable to respond to the music was frustrating him. He loved music and loved to dance. He could not have visitors the remainder of the day because he needed to rest.

Dr. Pencek, the neurosurgeon, came in to check on Joe and said that it was critical that he wake up. He said, "No sedation today because his blood pressure and heart rate are good."

Brian brought a stuffed dog in for Joe to rest his hand on, and the dog remained with him throughout his hospital stay.

People came to tell us that because of how Joe had touched their lives, they were going to change their life around for the better. One pastor even used Joe's accident for his sermon at church and titled it "Why Do Bad Things Happen to Good People?"

One day, Joe moved his right eyebrow for the first time; that was a huge step for him. He had not been able to move anything, except when he moved his hands and feet at the same time, and according to the doctor, that just wasn't medically possible. The doctors were not sure if he would ever move on his own again.

The man cleaning the hallway looked a lot like an actor I'd seen on TV, and when I turned to look at him again, he saw me. He left and came back later, so I told him I had looked at him because he reminded me of a TV actor. He just laughed. He saw me the next day in ICU and asked me who put the Psalm 91 on the wall in Joe's room, and I told him that I did. He then told me that it was his favorite psalm, so I told him that he could go into Joe's room anytime to read it, and he gave me a big hug. So many lives had been touched. Some people in our town had organized a benefit supper for Joe. Our hometown people were so caring and generous.

Thirteen days after the accident, Joe was moved out of ICU. He was breathing on his own, and they did another CT scan to compare to the one taken the night of the accident. The surgeon's nurse came by to see Joe and was surprised at the progress he had made. The scan still showed some swelling, but no bleeding, which was good news. Joe had started moving his eyes and his body more, which was progress. Every day was something new.

That Sunday, the boys and I decided to go to the Assembly of God church across the street from the hospital. I was having difficulty thinking about leaving Joe, but I heard there was a "More Lord" revival going on at the church, and I for sure needed more of the Lord like never before. It was a great service and just what I needed. When we got back to the hospital, Joe's blood pressure was good, his temperature was down, the feeding tube was working, and he was breathing on his own, with no help from the machine. Toni was there with Joe and asked him to squeeze her hand, and he did, so she asked him again, and he did it again. That was a big step for him.

On the fifteenth day after the accident, Joe's nurse told me that she was a born-again Christian and said everyone was talking about how the surgeon was giving God all the glory for Joe and for bringing him through. She said that God sometimes humbled doctors to show them that He's in control. Shortly after speaking with her, a woman from social services came in to check on Joe; she told me that he had been on her mind and she had been lifting him up in prayer all weekend.

As I was walking down the hall, I saw Joe's day nurse again, and she asked me if I knew where the chapel was. I said that I did and told her about the service there with the group from Pensacola and how excited the chaplain was.

She said to me, "See, another life has been changed and touched by Joe, and your basket isn't even full yet. You have quite a story to tell."

The ENT doctor told me that Joe may need facial surgery, but he explained that he had an advantage, since the sinus cavity by Joe's right eye was so small, it was not damaged by the tree limb. He also discussed putting a feeding tube in Joe's stomach and performing a tracheotomy in his throat to get the tubes out of his mouth. As he was talking, he began to mix into the conversation that he had been listening to a message by a pastor the night before, and he had spoken about going through trials and tribulations.

He said that the apostle Paul asked God to remove the thorn from his flesh, and God said, "My grace is sufficient for thee."

The doctor then told me that he wanted me to rely on God's grace because with a head injury, you never know the outcome, but with God, we do know that He is all knowing and in control.

He said, "Please do not forget that." How great was it that this doctor was talking to me about God?

Later that evening, Joe began gasping for air, and the nurse went to get the respiratory therapist. The tubes were taken out of Joe's mouth, and they began to bag him. We learned that he had some mucous in his airway, but they were able to remove it with the bag. He then began to spike a fever, and blood was drawn to see what was causing the fever. I was told that something like mucous in the airway can be very traumatic, but somehow, he calmed down through the night.

Things seemed better the next day. Joe was making more facial movements, and when the doctor shined the light in Joe's eyes, he would move them. He asked Joe to blink, but this was very hard for him, and it seemed as if he was trying to use every muscle in his face to do it. Just then, it looked like his left eye was trying to open a little. He also began to move his left arm and his feet.

I asked Joe to squeeze my hand with his right hand, and he was able to do that. I asked him to do that two more times, and he did; he didn't want to let go. That was amazing. As we were doing this, the internal medicine doctor came in and said he wanted to remove the TPN tube out of Joe's vein, where the nutrients and proteins were going in. Instead, he wanted the feeding tube to be turned up from sixty drips a minute to a hundred drips. It was so important for Joe to get nutrients to survive.

Rich, our friend who came to pray through the night for Joe, came to see us again and told me that he had received a word from the Lord for me. He said that this word came to him three different times, but each time was the same. He explained that the Lord had said, "Rest in what has already been done. The healing has already taken place, but Joe has not yet received the miracle. I am taking time to prepare Joe."

I was so touched that I couldn't seem to do anything but cry.

Sam, our pastor, and his wife, Judy, also came by to see us that day; he anointed Joe's eyes and said, "According to your faith let it be done unto you."

Joe had an unending amount of faith.

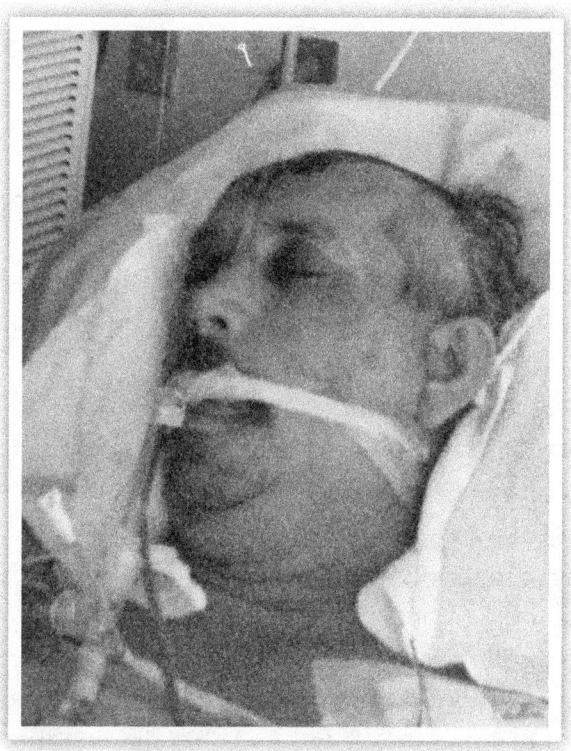

CHAPTER 5

The stories keep coming to me about lives that had been touched by Joe. A friend of ours who was visiting a church in Indiana called and said that during praise and worship, a lady went up to the microphone and called the church to prayer for Joe (our friend didn't know who that lady was). She said that a prayer began for Joe, and it was heavenly, and another lady came up to our friend and told her that her friend Joe was going to be fine. I continued to be amazed at how this accident had touched so many lives.

Sixteen days after the accident, the doctor wanted us to keep trying to wake Joe up. It seemed impossible to do, and I was thinking it was just not the right time. After all, God did tell me that He was preparing Joe. There had been so many dreams and visions happening at the same time, so it told me that God was up to something big.

A friend of mine called and said that she was listening to the song "We Will Ride," and in her spirit, she could tell that it meant something different this time. She asked God to tell her what the song meant because she knew it was something to do with Joe. In her spirit, she heard God say to her, "The fire in My eyes is My love for Joe and Peggy."

She could see dark clouds in the sky, with the sun's rays behind them. She could not see the sun but could see the brightness of the sun. The clouds were the darkness that happened to Joe, but the light shining through was the glory coming through the darkness, glory that was taking place in our lives. I looked at this as another message from God.

I sat at Joe's bedside and decided to see if he could hear me. Many people had asked if Joe could hear us. I told Joe that if he could hear me, on the count of three, he should open his eyes. His eyes did not open, but he tried to raise both eyelids at the same time. He was trying so hard, and I was so proud of him.

The mail came while I was sitting with Joe, and we received a very touching letter from Jason, the teenaged son of our close friends, Eric and Liz.

This was what the letter said:

> God, please heal Thy servant Joe. Whom happenstance conspired to bring low. He lies there in bed, trapped in his head, unable to find his way out. So, give him a light, to lead from his plight and send all the demons in rout. Please break every fetter, till he's never been better, and even the most stubborn can't doubt that it's all by your hand and follows Your plan and the wicked can do nothing but pout.
>
> Father in heaven, show mercy on Thy son. Reach out Thy hand and raise Joseph up from his sickbed so that he might praise Thee and give glory to Thy holy Name, in assembly and out, by himself and in the presence of multitudes.
>
> Holy Spirit, by Thy power, heal and awaken Joe. Bring him back, not just to the state he was in before, but make him stronger yet. Let him be a witness to the glory and power of the Spirit.
>
> Jesus, my Savior, heal one more man, as Thou hast done for so many others, as was done during Thy ministry and that of Thy disciples. Intercede with the Heavenly Father, that He might show mercy on His servant. With Thy blood cover his iniquities and sins, healing him with the same touch.

This I pray in the name of the Lord Jesus Christ, the son of God, who died and rose again, giving His own life as sacrifice for the sin of all who accept Him and who is my own personal Savior. Amen.

Wow. So many lives were being touched; this letter was from a teenager who wanted desperately for God to heal Joe. I was so thankful that this young man's life was being touched in a special way. This young man, as we could see, had an amazing relationship with our God.

Eighteen days after the accident, the respiratory doctor wanted to start weaning Joe off the respirator; there was also discussion about placing a tracheal tube, so we began to pray specifically that Joe would not have to have one inserted. I asked Joe to squeeze my hand, and he did, and he opened his left eye a little bit; it seemed like he was trying to see. I noticed that his upper lip moved just a little bit, like he was trying to smile. Could he be trying to wake up?

Joe's internist was great; when he would come into Joe's room, he would talk to him, and he was impressed that day when Joe squeezed his hand. Joe has always had a strong handshake. The doctor said that he believed that Joe was moving right along; those were encouraging words, and as he was leaving, he said, "Joe may receive another miracle today and will not need the tracheal tube placed after all." Joe's doctors were even expecting God to move for Joe.

Dr. Pencek came in to check on him; they were taking him off several medications, and he wanted Joe to wake up. He was very pleased with his progress but wanted a feeding tube placed in his stomach as soon as possible. He wanted him on liquid food because he felt like Joe was dwindling down to nothing. He also noticed that Joe's liver enzyme level was elevated, but there was no report that explained why.

Later that day, Joe's mom came to visit and spend some time with him. She asked Joe to put up one finger, two fingers and then three fingers, and he did it. She then asked Joe how many children he had, and he put up two fingers, which was correct. She also asked him who got the stuffed puppy for him, and he put up two fingers for number two son, Brian, which was also correct. He was for sure hearing us, and now, it seemed like he was trying to communicate in another way. I was so happy that day.

Just as he began to come around, he had a really bad episode. His breathing became very labored and rapid, and the machine alarms went off; his nurses came running, and his internist came in. They pulled out his respirator tube and inserted another one. That was so hard on Joe because he had been on that machine for so long now. Joe's throat was full of mucous, his temperature was 105, and his hemoglobin count was up to 12. They were going to do a bronchoscopy to see where the mucous was coming from. His blood pressure was now 101/57, and his heart rate was too high at 135. They gave him an antibiotic and Tylenol for the fever. They were not sure if he aspirated something into a lung or had pneumonia, but his lungs were clear. An x-ray was taken and showed a small amount of pneumonia in the right lung; they also wanted to take pictures of his legs to check for blood clots.

Joe had calmed down, and the doctor told Tony and me to go to our room to get some rest; one of our best friends, Larry, stayed with Joe and said that he'd call if they needed anything from me. I did get a call at eleven o'clock, and I needed to go back. Tony and I returned to the hospital. Joe needed to have a Greenfield filter put in to catch the blood clots that were in his legs. I needed to sign the consent to have the procedure done.

He had been wearing wraps around his legs to prevent the clots, but he now needed the filter. He was scheduled to have a titanium filter inserted in his umbilical area with a tube. The respiratory x-ray also showed that he had a small blood clot in his left lung, but that wasn't a problem. We waited while they did the procedure and went back to the hotel around three in the morning, after it was completed. The days and nights were definitely running together.

I lay in bed but couldn't go to sleep, again. I kept telling myself that I had to look beyond what I was seeing and feeling. I began to ask myself if I was strong enough to get through this and for what our lives were going to be. I told myself over and over that I could not give up; I had to tell myself that I had to stand on what I believed to be true and not to let go of God. I cannot tell you how many times thoughts of giving up entered my mind; that's what Satan wanted me to do, but I could not stay in those thoughts.

A very real spiritual battle was taking place, and I knew if Satan could get me where he wanted me, then I would give up on Joe. I had to keep my eyes and my thoughts on God and praise Him and thank Him for what He was doing in Joe. I could not miss what God was doing in and through Joe. This made me remember something that I had read somewhere. When you put God in His rightful place in your life, He will put you in your rightful place. He will provide for you there and protect you there. It made me aware of the feeling of a covering over me and Joe and Tony and Brian because there was no other way we could be in this place.

Many, many times, I lean close to Joe and whisper in his ear, "Are you in there somewhere?" I knew that he was in there but just could not get out. Yet.

Dr. Pencek's nurse came in to see Joe and said that the doctor wanted us to talk to Joe that day and let him know that we were in the room with him, but that was all to be done that day; we could not work with him much. She suggested that I have the nurses at the nurse's station help me control the number of visitors. Things needed to slow down.

Dr. Baker came in to see Joe and said that he already knew the answer but had to ask if Joe was a drinker, and I told him that he was not. He said that he could tell because of my walk with my God. He then told me that he really enjoyed the Christian music that was playing in Joe's room; I was amazed at how many times this doctor mentioned God.

Remember the custodian I previously told you about? Well, he came down to Joe's room to see me. He wanted to know how Joe was doing and told me that he prayed for Joe and me every night, and when he did, a "calming peace" came over him. That was so sweet of him; I was excited to get to talk to him again.

Marlene, my sister-in-law, came to visit; she hugged me and whispered, "Do not forget that there are times when God moves suddenly." She was standing at Joe's bedside, praying in the spirit, and she just kept hearing the words, "God moves suddenly and in His time." I truly hung onto those words. She also told me that when she prayed for Tony and Brian right after the accident, God told her that Tony was receiving a portion of Joe's love for God and that a spiritual renewal would be seen in him.

After I left to go to the chapel, things really started happening with Joe. His heart rate went way up, and the monitors were all going off. Larry was with Joe because we never wanted him to be alone, so he went to the nurse's station to get help, but they were already on their way to the room. The respiratory therapist came and began to use the suction tube; he noticed that Joe seemed more stressful. Joe had been turned earlier, so they thought that might have put his body in more stress. His blood pressure continued to go up, so Larry stood at the foot of Joe's bed and asked God's angels to protect Joe. The respiratory therapist turned on the machine that did the breathing for Joe, so he could rest. They repositioned him again, and that seemed to help; his numbers began to go back down. I was told that the blood clot that was thrown to the lung yesterday may be causing all of this, or it may be an infection. More blood work and tests were ordered, and we'd wait to see if he was sent back to ICU.

Larry didn't know whether to call me or not. He prayed over Joe, and each time that he thought about calling me, he heard a voice say to him, "Oh, ye of little faith," so he decided to relax and let God do His work. He later told me that Joe's accident had truly opened his eyes and pulled him out of a "back-row" attitude. He said that we all go through down times, and in the last few months, he felt that he was not in good favor with God. He seemed to have a nonchalant attitude. He said that he was sure that he was the one that stepped back and not God. He told me that he was drawing so much strength from me. This strength that seemed to be following me around was hard to explain, but it always seemed to be with me. God tells us in His Word that He will never leave us or forsake us.

Another friend of ours, Eric, called and wanted to share with me something that God had shown him. God showed him that this accident was like a web, and a web is one of the strongest things around; it is stronger than any other substance. Many of these people knew each other, but many did not; they had nothing in common except praying for Joe. Hundreds and thousands of people praying everywhere in one accord. Acts 1:14 says, "They all joined together constantly in prayer." And Acts 4:23 says, "They raised their voices together in prayer to God." I was so thankful that he shared this with me.

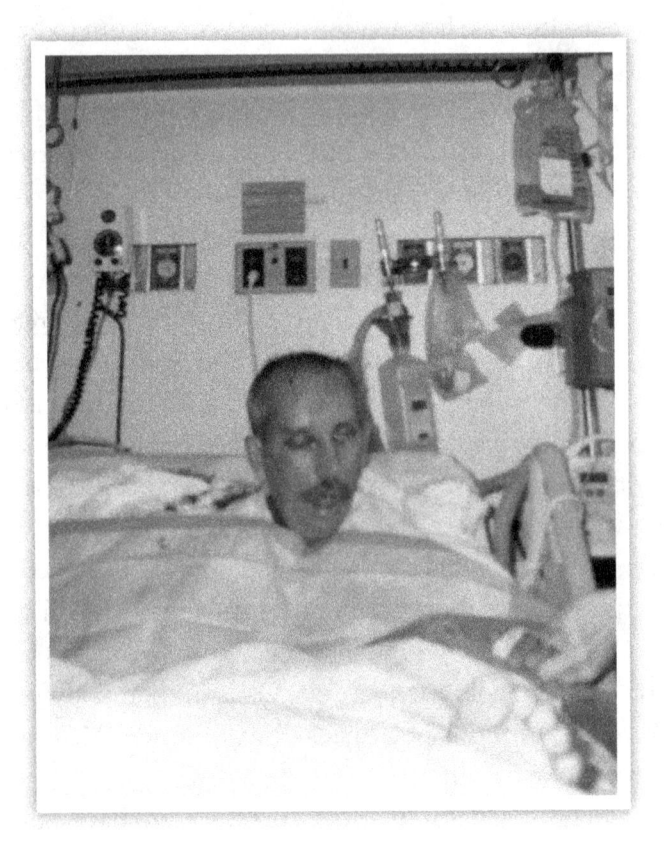

CHAPTER 6

It was the middle of March now, and I was so excited to see Joe's left eye opening a little bit more, and he was trying to follow people around the room. He smiled at me today for the first time, and I had to blink the tears from my eyes. I was so excited, not just for me but for Joe. He started squeezing hands that day too. Dr. Baker came in to see him and asked Joe to blink once for "yes" and twice for "no." He then asked Joe if he understood, but instead of blinking his eyes, he nodded his head yes. The doctor and I just looked at each other because we were so surprised. I then asked Joe if he could put his hand on the stuffed puppy that was lying next to him, and he did. He was sure working hard that day. Since he had a rough time the night before, we were all amazed at what he was able to do. Once the word got out to the nurses and his other doctors, they started coming in to see what Joe was able to do. No one expected him to ever be able to do these things again. It was a happy day.

The CT scan that was taken earlier came back fine, so the doctors were still not sure why other tests were showing the bottom and back of his lungs relaxing. It possibly could have been because he had been lying on his back for so long. There was currently no pneumonia, and the liver enzyme stats were normal. I thought I should tell myself that the reports from the doctors were catching up with the report of the Lord.

I heard that Pastor Sam started the Sunday service with Joe's story. He said that he had referred to Joe several times since the accident, but what was it about Joe that was so unique? He said that Joe was always a happy guy and had this excitement that seemed to surround him. He said that he liked to look at Joe when he preached because Joe was not only "spirit filled" but was also "spirit spilled." I couldn't wait to share with Joe what the pastor said.

The physical therapist came in the next day to try to get Joe to bend his legs and to hold his arms up at his elbows. You see, Joe could not move anything on his own. His body would have to be taught how to do everything again. He could do nothing by himself at this point. The therapist wanted us to work with Joe, so she showed us some treatments to do with him. He was trying to move his head and seemed to be trying to nod, and we kept trying to help him.

The surgeon also came in to check on Joe and was very pleased with his progress. He explained that he had to insert several pieces of titanium in his head to replace the skull that was damaged. He said that he was hoping not to have to put Joe through another surgery, but if it did happen, it would only be in the occipital area. He also said that Joe's white cell count had also been elevated, and it was because of a blood clot in one of his lungs, so he would be given an antibiotic. The ENT doctor came in to tell us that Joe may or may not need facial surgery; we'd have to wait and see.

It was another day now, and Scott, one of the pastors from our hometown, came to check on Joe and me, and he was amazed. He told me that he couldn't wait to go back home and tell everyone how well Joe was doing. He said that when Lazarus was raised from the dead, the people were amazed and hurried to tell others what happened. He said that this was how he felt, an urgency to tell others.

Shortly after Scott left, one of Joe's nurses came by to talk to me. She wanted to know exactly what happened to Joe. After I told her the story, she said that there was no way that Joe should be alive because the head injury was so severe and because it was a compound fracture. She was so touched by his story that she had tears in her eyes.

Just after she left, I started watching a pastor on TV who was speaking about the anointing and miracles, and I felt like he was speaking directly to me. He said that if you have the anointing, you have everything you need for your miracle. The anointing can give you everything you need. It was like the woman in the Bible who only had the oil. The oil was the anointing, and the prophet was preparing her for her miracle, so the woman got all her things together. He said that we need to stop thinking small. If we keep pouring, God will keep pouring. If we turn loose of what we have in our hand, God will turn loose of what He has in His hands. He said that you cannot get your miracle by looking in the rearview mirror and do not look at what you have as lack but as the beginning.

When I heard these words, it was like they penetrated my body. I knew what I had to continue doing. I could not and would not be able to handle each day without the anointing. I could not think that Joe wouldn't make it, and I kept believing that with God, all things are possible. I had to think big because He is a big God. I would focus on what I knew God could and would do and thank Him for the days yet to come.

I have to admit that there were days I'd be frustrated and wonder where God was because I could not seem to find Him. I would be so wrapped up in everything that was going on; so many doctors, nurses, wires, machines, and alarms going off. It was often overwhelming. I did not want my feelings to overtake my faith, and I did not want the circumstances around me to take over my life. I just wanted God to be God. I needed to stop and remember who was in control and know that He would deliver exactly what we needed and when we needed it.

It was the end of March now, and the doctors seemed very pleased with Joe's progress. They wanted to take him off the respirator as soon as they could. He was starting to try to move his hands more so when the surgeon's assistant came in, she asked Joe to move his thumbs and squeeze her hand. He was able to do both, and she was so happy. He also picked his right hand up off the pillow and put it on his stomach. Who would have thought that such a small movement would have made me cry?

It was not small; it was huge for Joe. I had to step out of the room for a minute to regroup because there were so many doctors, nurses, and medical students in his room. As I looked down the hall, I saw a friend of ours by the elevator, so I went over to him, and he asked if he could pray for Joe and me, so we joined hands and prayed. The timing was perfect.

When I got back to Joe's room, he had spiked a fever of over 102. It came up quickly, so his nurses started putting cold rags on his head to bring the fever down. The fever did not break until four hours later.

I was told that we needed to think about where Joe could have physical and occupational therapy. I checked with our insurance, and everything was still okay, but I found out that the therapy he needed couldn't be done at the hospital where he was. I was so disappointed because they had helped him so much here, and again, it felt like being with family.

One of Joe's doctors told me that I needed to think of a "facility" that I would like for Joe to be taken to. "Facility?" I had not given that word a thought. He told me because of the severity of the head injury that he would need to be taken somewhere and that I should not expect Joe to get any better than he was right now. When I asked him what therapy Joe would need, he told me I was expecting too much. Of course I was. I knew what my God could do, and I knew that He was not done with Joe. Philippians 1:6 says to be "confident that He who began a good work in us will carry it on to completion."

I decided then that I no longer wanted this doctor on Joe's case, and I didn't want any doctors who had given up on him. Just then, our youngest son, Brian, reminded me that in the book of Mark, Jesus got rid of the unbelievers before he raised Jairus's daughter from the dead. The boys and I prayed about this. Every day seemed to be like a new part of this journey. I knew that I had to look beyond what I was seeing and feeling. I needed to keep my eyes on God and who He was and what He was doing. Joe was lying in the hospital bed, not knowing anything that was happening.

I also remember the many times I heard Joe say, "It is okay with me for God to do whatever He needs to through me to further his kingdom." In 1 Timothy 1, it says, "I thank Christ Jesus our Lord, who has given me strength, that he considered me faithful, appointing me to His service." This was Joe. I knew that God was still on the move, so I had to keep my eyes on Him, and I did not want to miss what He was doing with and through Joe.

When I got to Joe's room the next day, one of my favorite doctors came in to see Joe; I was so thankful, and the timing was perfect. This doctor always came in and talked to Joe and me. It helped when he explained what he thought the other doctor was meaning about Joe's therapy. He told me that there were different places between the care that Joe was receiving now and a full rehabilitation center. He told me again that he believed that Joe was an answer to prayer. So when the other doctor came back to see Joe again, I asked him if I could speak to him outside of Joe's room. He followed me out, and I asked him what he meant about Joe being transferred to another facility. He then told me that the head injury was so severe that I would need to accept the fact that Joe was not going to get any better than where he was right then. That was not going to happen.

I told the doctor that I could not and would not believe that and if he didn't believe that Joe was going to get better, I didn't want him as one of Joe's doctors. I suggested that we go back into Joe's room and said he should speak to Joe and ask him if he could shake his hand. He had never spoken to Joe like that, so when we went back into the room, he leaned over the bed and told Joe who he was; Joe lifted his hand to shake the doctor's hand, and I wanted to cry so bad. We did not ask Joe to do that. He just did it. The doctor was rather surprised and just looked over at me.

The next day was a big day for Joe, even though his fever returned, but they were not sure why. Joe lifted his fingers off the pillow, did a high five with his right hand, waved at people, nodded his head yes and no, squeezed hands, and kept time with Christian music that was playing in his room. When Joe's nurse heard all of the commotion, she came into the room, and when she heard what was going on, she said, "Welcome back, Joe." She was so excited about what he was doing that she ran back out of the room to tell the other nurses. They came running too.

The pulmonary doctor also came in to check on Joe and said that things were looking good; he also said that Joe was the talk of the hospital. The internist also came in to see Joe; he checked the feeding tube, which was fine, and let us know that Joe's liver enzymes were stable. They weren't sure why they had been so high, possibly from medication or the TPN line in his clavicle.

The next day, when I got to the hospital, Joe's nurse came out to meet me in the hall and told me there was a small white dove sitting on the ledge outside Joe's window, looking inside; then she said, "It was not just any bird, you know; Joe just had a divine visitation." What a great thing to hear from Joe's nurse. So many people seemed to be able to see the way that God was showing up for Joe.

When Joe woke up on this day, he really woke up. He gave a thumbs-up, raised his hands to praise the Lord, counted with his fingers, squeezed hands, and moved his legs and feet when I asked him to. I also showed him pictures of our family and asked him to squeeze my hand if he knew who they were, and he did. He was doing so well that I asked the physical and occupational therapists if they could come back in to work with Joe, and they did. Joe did well for a little while but then couldn't do any more. They asked Joe if he was trying, and he shook his head no. They wore him out, and at least he was honest.

As Joe was napping, I looked back over everything that had happened, wondering if I should have done anything differently. I began to question some of the decisions I made. I called Mary, a friend of mine, to talk to her about my feelings. After a while, she told me about a Bible story where God said, "Do not look back or you will become like Lot's wife." The story tells us that when Lot's wife looked back to the city, she was turned into a pillar of salt.

I had to cut the conversation short because the doctor I spoke to earlier about putting Joe into a facility came over to talk to me. He said he didn't want me to think that he wanted to put Joe somewhere and forget about him. He said we needed to think of a therapy center, and I told him that I was already working on that. He then told me that Joe was making really good progress; each little step was progress, but the road would be long. I told him that we were considering moving Joe to a hospital in St. Louis that was equipped to help with brain injury patients.

Yay. Joe's right eye opened just a little bit. He was picking his right hand up and moving it more on his own. This was a huge step for him. He had had no control over anything, and his tongue just hung out of his mouth, but when we asked him to put his tongue in his mouth, he did it. This was another big step. The respirator may be taken off if Joe continued to breathe on his own. He was moving his hands and arms all over the place, with no one helping him. This had been a great, great day for Joe.

Joe's surgeon came in again and further discussed facial surgery, since his sinus had been cracked and his left jaw was broken. While we were waiting for x-rays to be ordered, the teacher from our Sunday school class came in; he told us that he would be putting Joe's name on next Sunday's attendance record. He told Joe that we had no idea how many people we taught about faith and the number of lives that had been touched by our story. It was great to hear and great to see him.

The occupational therapist came in to check on Joe's feet and to make splints for better support. The internist also came in and said that they were still watching Joe's liver enzymes; they were currently elevated but not dangerously high. I asked if the trauma from hitting his side on the bucket that he was in could have caused this; he said it was highly unlikely but not impossible.

The respiratory therapist also told us that Joe was receiving very little support from the breathing vent. A blood gas was drawn to make sure he could breathe on his own; I was so excited. I remember standing at the foot of Joe's bed in ICU and thanking God that he could breathe on his own, even though he was not. At that time, Joe looked like he would never breathe on his own again. I knew that

I had to look beyond what I was seeing and believe that God was bigger than this accident.

Several of us prayed for Joe before leaving for the night; one of my friends said that during the prayer, she could see two very large angels standing in Joe's room; one of them was holding a large staff in his hand. There was no doubt in my mind that God was protecting Joe.

It was getting closer to the time for Joe to start rehab; the respiratory doctor wanted to get the ventilation tube out of Joe's throat because it was harder for him to breathe with it in there. I was looking so forward to this happening.

When the internist came in, Joe, by himself, lifted his hand up like he wanted to shake the doctor's hand. The doctor took Joe's hand and told him that he wanted to ask him some questions, and he wanted him to blink once for yes and twice for no. I then told the doctor that Joe could nod for yes or no. The doctor was shocked and said, "Oh, okay." The doctor asked Joe if he was in any pain and Joe shook his head no. Joe would even tell you today that he has never been in any pain.

I then found out that a friend of ours had called the Christian radio station and asked them to pray for Joe. She had told them about the severity of the head injury, and that day, when we were listening to the radio, the announcer began telling Joe's story and asking listeners to pray for him. It was so wonderful to see how God was moving in so many different areas and in so many different directions.

On this night, Larry was staying with Joe so I could get some sleep; around 4 a.m., the humidified oxygen control made a very loud noise, and it woke Joe up. The nurse came in and replaced it, but Joe could not get back to sleep. So Larry asked him if he wanted to listen to some music, which Joe loves, and he nodded yes. Larry put some Christian music on, and Joe began to keep time with the music by tapping the fingers of his right hand. We were later told that Joe should not have been able to do that. Whenever we asked

Joe to praise the Lord, he would lift his arm up as best he could and move it back and forth.

I was also told by the pulmonary doctor that we needed to try to get Joe to wake up. That was still so important. He would not take the breathing tube out until Joe was awake more. We tried all that we could to get Joe to stay awake more, and it must have been enough because the breathing tube was removed; an oxygen mask would be used for a while to see how well he would do with it. Praise God.

CHAPTER 7

March 29, 1999, was four weeks after the accident. Joe was doing so well that the respiratory doctor took him completely off the oxygen. He told me that Joe was moving along a lot faster than anyone ever thought he would. It was only by prayer and the holy grace of God; every day, we are shown how amazing our God is.

Several of the doctors came in to see how Joe was doing; they were all amazed at his progress. I shook their hands and told them how much we appreciated everything they had done to help Joe. I told a couple of them that we would walk back in to see them, and their comment was, "We don't doubt that a bit."

Joe was starting rehab at a different facility, but before he left, he had one final CT scan to check all the fractures in his face. The scan was difficult for Joe because he had trouble breathing and had to be suctioned several times during the scan.

The scan showed several small fractures, with a major one from the right side of his nose up to his forehead. That one may need surgery for medical reasons, as it could allow cerebral fluid to leak. The other fracture of concern was in the bone under his left eye. When it started to mend, it didn't line up totally, but it would only need surgery for cosmetic reasons. The jaw fractures had healed. I asked the doctor because right after the accident, the surgeon told us he could pull the whole jaw area out; he was aware of the former CT scan and even questioned the radiologist to double-check the scan.

The radiologist said that there was no evidence of a jaw fracture ever being there. What a miracle. The jaw extended normally, and it was as though it never happened.

It may not sound like much, but each time Joe would do something, we'd get so excited because he was not supposed to be able to do anything for himself. He was squeezing people's hands, doing the "okay" sign with his fingers, waving at people, touching his nose, shaking people's hands, putting his fingers up for different numbers, and lifting his eyebrows, even though his right eye remained shut.

It had been a month now, and Joe was the talk of the hospital. It was time to transfer to a rehab center in St. Louis. This was a super hard step for us, and I had to make so many decisions that I didn't know if I could make another. I had never been the strong one in our relationship and always looked to Joe to make the big decisions, but this was a step that had to be taken for Joe to get better. So many people were coming in to see Joe because they knew he would be leaving in a couple of days. This was a time of sadness and joy. It was going to be hard to leave everyone who had been so wonderful to us, yet this would be another chapter in our lives. The book of Joshua says, "Do not be terrified, do not be discouraged, for the Lord your God will be with you wherever you go."

Joe was now off all medications and had been unhooked from all his monitors. Praise the Lord. I was becoming even more overwhelmed because of all the changes taking place. I cried a lot and felt a lot of anger because of what happened to Joe. I didn't understand why. Joe loves the Lord so much and would do anything for anybody. I just wanted our lives back. We had made it through so many trials with God's help, but this trial had been devastating. There were days when everything inside of me would hurt, way down deep in my soul. I had to stay strong, though, and had to keep trusting God. He must have bigger plans for us, and He would never leave us or forsake us. The Lord is our God. He is in control and is the master of our lives. Romans 8:28 says, "All things work together for the good of those who have been called according to His purpose."

We have been called by God to walk this walk, and I heard Joe say many times, "God can do anything He needs to do and can use me any way he wants to for His glory."

Joe was being moved to St. Louis the next day. I was so emotional. I knew that I could not go alone and make it through such a difficult time. Larry took the time to drive me there, and Toni stayed with Joe because I never wanted Joe to be alone. It was hard on me to see so many patients at the hospital in St. Louis with brain trauma and trying so hard to get better. There are so many stages of brain trauma that I saw that it was more than I could handle, and I just shook all over. It made me second-guess the decision to go there with Joe, but the hospital had agreed to accept Joe as a patient, so that was where we would go and put it all in God's hands.

While Toni was with Joe and before I got back to the hospital, she said that Joe took her hands in his and moved them back and forth across his face. She felt like Joe was wondering how his face must look. Just typing these words makes me cry. I cannot imagine how Joe must have been feeling on the inside and not being able to speak. She then began to tell Joe how the fractures in his face were healing and how his upper and lower jaw was broken, and that God healed them. She then told him about going to St. Louis for rehab and how it was going to be a lot of hard work, and Joe nodded his head. I can't keep typing right now; this is so hard to relive.

I'm back. Sometimes, I just can't fight off the emotions as I tell this story. It feels like it was just yesterday.

Later that afternoon, Joe had his mouth closed and was breathing through his nose. I was not sure that was what I was hearing, so I got closer to listen, and he was; he had not been able to do that before. This was another huge step for him. When the respiratory therapist came in to check him, we were told that the bottom of Joe's lungs were becoming relaxed because of laying down for so long; that was not a good sign.

Several tests and breathing treatments were done before we would leave. Joe's liver enzymes were still elevated, but there seemed to be no medical reason for it. My favorite doctor came to see us before we left and told me that Joe had surprised everybody with his progress, and he said that he knew Joe would walk back in to see him someday. The speech therapist also came in to check on Joe and said that the feeding tube would need to stay in longer until Joe was awake more. She tried to get Joe to move his tongue from side to side and up and down, but he could not. Seemed like something so simple to do and not to think about having to do, but Joe just could not do it. Yet.

There was still some concern by the doctors about the facial fractures, especially the fracture through the right sinus. The doctor said that roughly 10 percent of people have a small sinus like Joe's. The backbone of the sinus was separated, and the bone can grow back over the separation, and that would be great. If that did not happen, we would need to be concerned about cranial fluid leakage and possible meningitis. So we pray "bone to bone and flesh to flesh."

Joe would be taken to St. Louis by ambulance, and I could not go with him. He was being made ready for the trip, so I left to try to get a head start on the trip. I needed to stop by our house; I had not been home for a month. As I walked out of Joe's room, the nurses and doctors were lined up in the hallway to say goodbye. Tears were running down my face and some of their faces too; it was a time I will never forget.

Mary and Toni were with me when I left the hospital and made the trip to our house with me. When we got to our house, I could hardly open the door, I was shaking so badly and crying so hard. I had this overwhelming feeling that nothing in this home would ever be the way it was. I think I was so scared, and I had not really felt like this before. With everything I had dealt with so far, I just had not experienced this feeling.

My friends and I walked through the house, and we were all crying and praying and believing that God would take care of us when we came back home. It was such a struggle to realize that our lives would never be the same and we were in a place that we didn't want to be. But God knew where we were, and He was teaching us in this struggle, so I had to keep looking for the miracles. I'll never forget how I felt that day, and as I type, I can feel those same feelings. I knew that I had to pull myself together and get to the hospital to be with Joe.

Joe and I had made it this far, so I knew we could go farther.

CHAPTER 8

Everything was different now. Everybody was different now too. It seemed strange to me that there was no one checking on Joe frequently. I felt like I was the only one making sure that he was okay; I was used to so many people being around him. Here, hours went by without any nurse or anyone coming in. So as I sat there with Joe, I did a lot of thinking. For some reason, God had given us this walk to walk. One thing that I did know for sure was that I still put all my hope and trust in God.

Since we were at a new place, the therapists wanted me to show them what Joe had been able to do. It was good to find out that what we had been doing together was what would have been done if we had been at this hospital. The therapist then sat Joe up on the side of the bed, which had never been done, and he found out that Joe could not hold himself in any position. The therapist even had to hold Joe's head up because he could not do it on his own. He had lost all ability to control anything on his body on his own. He could not even hold saliva in his mouth because he could not close his mouth.

The therapist wanted to check his awareness, so she brought in things to smell: coffee, cinnamon, and vanilla. He didn't really respond to any of them except the coffee.

A special chair was ordered since he had lost all his muscle function. When it arrived, he was sat in that chair, but he looked like a paraplegic. He could not hold any part of his body up on his own. He was left in the chair for a few hours, which seemed like a long time to me, since he had not done this before. I went to ask someone how long he should be sitting up, and someone came to put him back in bed.

We were also told that we could not stay with Joe at this hospital. I was not happy at all. Joe had not been alone since the accident, and I didn't want to leave him then, but I had no choice. The boys and I got a room close to the hospital, and we could walk to get back there (quickly, if need be).

When we got to the hospital early the next morning, Joe had spiked a fever. We were told that he could not do therapy until the fever was gone. We were also told that chest x-rays, urine test, and blood test had been done. Tony and I started putting cold rags on Joe's head. We didn't know what else to do. After a time, his temperature did go back down. I decided it was a good time to read the Bible to Joe, which I had been doing since we were at the other hospital, and I knew this was one of the most important things I could do for him. Joe would read the scriptures every day, so I did not want that to stop.

Later that day, Joe started coughing and could not stop. I had been taught how to suction his throat, so I began doing that. It didn't help. Joe couldn't breathe. Toni was visiting that day and she and I started yelling for a nurse and pushing the alarm button, but no one came. Toni took off to find someone; she banged on the door of the nurse's room and yelled at them that Joe was choking. They came running. Joe's heart rate had shot up and his temperature too. They put Joe on oxygen, inserted an IV, and moved him to ICU. His heart rate stayed high at 142, and his temperature was hovering at 103. A cooling blanket was put under him to try to cool him down. The doctor was not sure about the cause; she considered trauma, infection, or possible brain damage from the head injury that had not occurred yet. We continued to pray. Joe continued to stay in ICU.

The next day was Easter Sunday, so the boys and I thought it best to go to our home church and call more saints to prayer for Joe. Everyone was so excited to see us; they had a thousand questions about Joe. Our church family had done so much for us; I think I cried through most of the service. It just felt so good to be there but so different without Joe.

When we got back to the hospital to check on Joe, his heart rate and temperature had gone down. I was told that it just went down that morning. Of course, it was Resurrection Sunday. Things really began to happen on that day. I asked Joe if he wanted a kiss, and he nodded yes. I gave him a kiss. He was trying to move his lips, which had never happened, like he wanted to give me a kiss. I put my cheek next to his lips and could faintly feel his lips move. It was so sweet. For some reason, his arms and hands were moving all over the place, nonstop.

Then I thought, *Let's just try something different for him.* I asked him what comes after the number five. He put up five fingers on one hand and one finger on the other hand. That was unbelievable. He had not even been able to raise his hands up before like he did this time. I just could not believe what was happening, but then I remembered what Marlene had told me about God moving suddenly.

I decided to help Joe put his arms around me, and I could tell that he was trying so hard to hug me. It had been a long, long time since I had felt one of his hugs. He even tried to rub my hair. Wow. Maybe he remembered being a hairdresser. I was trying to think of things that would help him remember; he loved to tell stories. Some were true, but some he made up, and they were so believable that you'd think they were true. So I asked him if he would tell me some stories, and he nodded his head yes. I asked him if he made some stories up, and he nodded his head yes again.

I was still so amazed. He could do none of this before, not even yesterday. He was put into ICU yesterday. As soon as the nurse saw all that he was doing, she said, "Joe is definitely in there." She was amazed at Joe's responsiveness to me. We had not experienced any of that since the head injury. If only Joe's brain surgeon could see him now.

He kept trying to sit up, which he had not tried on his own before. I thought all of this was probably wearing him out; I didn't want another setback, so I asked him if he wanted to go to sleep, but he just shrugged his shoulders like he didn't really care. I was sitting next to him and holding his hands, and he was squeezing my hands so tight that I had to ask him to stop. All of this was amazing, but I decided to leave because I really wanted him to rest. That had been an exciting day for him and for me, so as I was leaving, I told him goodbye, which I had never done, and he waved goodbye with his hand. I stepped out of the door and just began to cry. I truly believed with all my heart that God had resurrected him.

Pastor Sam came to see us the next day; Joe was very alert, and our pastor was so excited. He anointed Joe with oil and prayed, and Joe lifted both of his arms up to worship God. We didn't even ask him to do that. We both had tears in our eyes, and Pastor said that the anointing would enhance what we were already gifted to do. What an awesome thought. Two other pastors came in that day; we didn't even know them, but some people had asked them to come and pray with us. That was amazing.

Joe had recovered from what was determined to be aspiration in his lungs. The therapist said that it was important to get his therapy going. The first thing was to get good tennis shoes for him to wear through the day. He seemed to sleep a lot until midafternoon, but when he would wake up, he would be very alert. He would reach for me, and I would ask him if he wanted a hug, and he would nod his head yes. I would give him a hug and a kiss.

I felt like the time had come for me to really talk to Joe; I was hoping that he'd be able to understand what I was going to say. I told him things that had happened since the accident and what he had been through. I talked to him for a long time about how hard he was going to have to work so we could go home. He nodded yes and then went to sleep.

I also spoke to Joe's contact person at the hospital. She checked in to see how things were going, so I shared my concerns with her, and she assured me that he was in the right place for rehab. The Springfield hospital was just not equipped for this type of head injury. I did feel better, and Joe and I continued to work hard together.

There were not as many visitors now. Where we were was a farther drive for family and friends to come over, but my sister, Susie, drove over to the hospital every Sunday, even on Easter. She did not want me to be alone. When others did come, though, they were amazed at Joe's progress and could tell that he had been working hard.

One evening, our friends Mark and Denise came over to see us; Joe and I were listening to a Brownsville Revival CD, and when they stepped into the room, they started singing too. I looked at Joe, and he was trying to move his mouth to sing. I heard a noise come out of his mouth. He was trying to sing and we were all clapping for him. Tony came in and was so excited to see his dad trying to sing.

Mark and Denise offered to stay with Joe so I could rest; Tony and I left to go to the hotel. On the way, Tony told me that he had a dream about his dad. The two of them were in a room somewhere, and Tony remembered that Joe had a short haircut, like he did now, and he said that Joe was hugging him really tight; he said that Joe seemed just like the Joe that he used to be. I knew that the boys missed their dad and wanted him to be the father they always had. Sometimes, when I look at the boys or hear them talk about something like Tony did, I can tell that God is being so kind and doing a mighty work in them, but I also know that they truly miss their dad.

When we got to the hospital the next morning, Joe's breathing was labored, and I could tell that something was different. The respiratory therapist came in and said that this sleep pattern was neurological. His legs seemed to be swollen more too because of a blood clot. The physical therapist said that we needed to exercise it more. So I did what I could to help and did leg exercises with him when he was not in therapy.

Later in the day, I got out some of the cards that had been sent to Joe. There are so many of them that we couldn't keep all of them with us. I would read the card to him and tell him who it was from and then ask Joe if he knew who that person was, and he would nod his head yes. I would whisper into Joe's ear and say, "Are you in there somewhere?" I know now that Joe was in there somewhere.

The more that Joe was able to do, the more I could see the hand of God on him and all around him. There was no way Joe would be where he was today if it were not for God. Psalm 27:13–14 says, "I am still confident of this: I will see the goodness of the Lord in the land of the living. Wait for the Lord, be strong and take heart and wait for the Lord."

Joe began to be able to sit on the side of the bed without much help. He could kick his feet up and hold his head up better, and he smiled more. He tried to reposition himself in the bed too. He somehow used his elbows and feet and pushed himself back up. One day, Dick came to see Joe, and when he walked into the room, Joe's face lit up. We could tell that he was so happy to see Dick S. Joe seemed to be moving around a lot in the bed, so Dick asked him if he was uncomfortable, and we heard Joe say, "Little bit."

Dick and I gave each other a surprised look and said, "Did he just say something?" It had been a very long time since we had heard any words come out of Joe's mouth.

Brian was with us that day and could see what Joe could do. He saw his dad scratch his head, move his legs all over, pull on the bar over his bed, and clap his hands. He surprised us by taking my hand and putting it on his mouth, as if to kiss the back of my hand. It was so touching; I told him that when he squeezed my hand three times, that would mean "I love you." So every so often, he would squeeze my hand three times. He remembered what I had told him, so when he would do that, I knew he was saying, "I love you." It was the only way he could communicate.

When it was time for Brian to leave, he leaned over to give his dad a kiss; Joe put his arm around his neck and gave him a hug. Brian and I both started crying. It was still so hard to leave Joe at night, and I really didn't want to. But that night, as I lay in bed and closed my eyes, I could see this spiritual battle raging. It was going back and forth; Satan was trying to take Joe, but it was not happening. God kept protecting Joe, time and time again. Psalm 20 says, "May the Lord answer you when you are in distress; may He send you help from the sanctuary and grant you support from Zion."

I could tell that Joe was wanting to work hard to get better; it seemed like he was beginning to understand more. I thought I would take a chance and see how Joe would respond, so I asked him what 2 times 5 was, and he put up five fingers and then another five fingers. I must have had a surprised look on my face, but I clapped my hands to let him know that he was correct.

The physical therapists continued to come in and help Joe sit up more. He had been trying to get himself dressed, putting on shorts and a t-shirt. They actually got him to wipe his own mouth with a rag. The therapist asked me to work with Joe's legs more so that she could concentrate on other areas. Pastor Sam came in during Joe's therapy and was amazed to see him sitting up by himself. I was reminded of Proverbs 3:5–6: "Trust in the Lord with all your heart and lean not on your own understanding; in all your ways acknowledge him, and he will make your paths straight. Do not be wise in your own eyes; fear the Lord and shun evil. This will bring health to your body and nourishment to your bones."

We did not know how it was that Joe was able to do what he could do at this time, except that we serve an awesome God, and Joe is a child of the Most High. God is faithful to those who serve Him and call upon His name.

Pastor Sam told Joe a story about how his lawnmower was broken, and he needed to mow his yard. I looked at Joe and said, "You would help Pastor Sam, wouldn't you?"

Joe snapped his fingers on his right hand (as best he could), as if to say, "in a heartbeat," and then he did the same with his left hand. Pastor then leaned over to hug Joe, and Joe hugged him back and tried to say, "I love you." Pastor had tears running down his cheeks.

Joe really couldn't do much of anything with his mouth, but he sure was trying. The speech therapist wanted him to work on his smile, puckering his lips, and moving his tongue up and down, things we don't even have to think about doing, but he had to think hard to accomplish it. We could see by the look on his face that he was really trying.

The physical therapist said she was thinking about trying to get him ready to walk. When Joe heard her say that, he picked his right arm up and tried to make a fist and a thumbs-up, like he was ready to get started. After the therapist left, I asked if Joe could go outside in his chair, and they said it was fine. He had not been outside since March 1, the day of the accident. He loved it and held his head up by himself the whole time we were out there. It was a great time.

One day, Joe got to put his eyeglasses on; what a huge step for him. The occupational therapist wanted him to try to see words and objects on paper. She first asked Joe to point to his nose, leg, and shoulder and to make a fist to see how he would do. She then drew some designs, numbers, and letters on a sheet of paper and asked him to point to certain ones. She then wrote a sentence and asked him to point to the second word in the sentence. He was able to do it with a little help. She asked him what his last name was, and he told her that too. She told us that the better he did with speaking and swallowing, the sooner he could eat. That would be another huge step.

The recreational therapist came in to talk to Joe and ask him questions about what he liked to do; he tried to get Joe to write his name, but he couldn't do it. Yet.

I asked Joe if he wanted to go outside again for a while; he loved to be there. While we were outside, a loud siren went off, and Joe started moving his hands in a strange way. I asked him if the loud noise bothered him, and he nodded yes, so we went back to his room.

So much was happening. We found out that some of the people in our small town were planning an auction for our family, and the building where it would be held was provided free of charge. What a wonderful blessing. Roger, the owner of the building had been having a very difficult time whenever he thought about Joe's accident. He had been afraid that he was not going to survive, and he thought so much of Joe.

I was also told that one of the nurses on duty the night of Joe's accident had come across the x-rays that had been taken the night of the head injury; she said that there was no way that Joe should be able to do anything or to even be alive. I said, "Only by the grace of God and because of all of the prayers that have bombarded heaven for Joe."

The next day, we received some really good news. Joe's doctor came in to see him and was thrilled with his progress. She listened to his lungs and heart, and all was good. She moved his legs, and his range of motion was excellent. She said she originally thought Joe might have been moved to this therapy hospital too soon, but then he was in ICU last week, and she told me that had been a blessing because now he was really ready for rehab.

The therapist came in a little later and had Joe try to stand up. He stood up for five minutes and then got himself back into a chair. That was a first for him too. The physical therapist decided to take him to the rehab gym and have him stand up at the parallel bars; she got him to take five steps. She told me that her goal for him was four weeks. Wow. There seemed to be something new every day and he was doing so much.

The speech therapist asked Joe if she could ask him more questions and some harder than before. He nodded his head like he was ready. He scored a 90 percent on the simple questions and an 85 percent on the harder ones. She was thrilled with his progress.

The therapists were working him pretty hard. The occupational therapist had Joe sit on a table and try to hit a balloon back and forth; she then had him move his arms across the table as if he was wiping it table off. She began to tell him about the scars on his forehead and about his short haircut. She asked him if he wanted to look in the mirror, and he said, "No."

Then it was time for him to go back to his room to rest. When we thought he was asleep, Tony and I noticed that he was pulling at his sheets more than normal. Tony asked him if he had to go to the bathroom, and Joe nodded yes. Tony ran out to get the nurse, but she didn't make it in time. We were so excited that Joe figured out a way to get our attention because he needed to go.

On some days, Joe could not do therapy because he was so tired. He would try but kept falling asleep so not much was accomplished.

After just a couple of days, though, Joe walked down the parallel bars twice. That same day in speech therapy, he was asked to do some very difficult things, but he went through them with flying colors. She asked him to do three things in order, like point to her, point to the ceiling, and then point to the floor. She then asked him to stick his tongue out and touch his chin three times. Then she asked Joe to say his name, and we actually heard his voice. It had been a long time since we had heard his real voice. God kept filling our hearts with hope and joy.

Brian came in while Joe was still in therapy, and Joe kept pointing to the window, wanting Brian to know that he should take him outside. They couldn't go until therapy was done, but they did get to go after that, and it was so nice getting to see them spend time together.

The more I would see Joe do, the more I really missed him. Every minute was precious.

Later in the day, the nurses decided to put a urinal on Joe. They wanted to see if he could go to the bathroom on his own. If not, he would have to go back to a catheter. After several hours, they came back in to check on Joe, and he had gone on his own. I know that it seems like something simple, but it was not. This was a great step for him. Small steps back to his life.

The next day, when Joe was in therapy, a lady came in to see if she could help; the therapist introduced her to Joe, and she told him that she was a hairdresser. Joe shook her hand and smiled really big, one hairdresser to another.

When we got back to Joe's room, his phone rang, and it was a close friend of ours; I put the phone to Joe's ear, and he kept smiling. He loved to talk to people, so he was sure enjoying himself. Toni and Larry came to see Joe, and when they walked into the room, Toni said, "Did you miss me, Joe?" and he very clearly said, "No." It was so funny because it was so like Joe to be a teaser, and we all laughed so hard.

I wanted Joe to see some of the cards that had been sent to him; most of them were from the schools in our hometown. I was trying to tell him which grade that I thought they were from, and he kept correcting me, and come to find out, he was right. He always used to tell me that he was always right. He used to say, "Peggy, just say the word, 'r i g h t.'"

I used to say, "I can't say that word." It was hilarious.

He was able to do more each day. He loved waving at everyone he saw, whether he knew them or not, and he loved shaking people's hands. That was so much like Joe. He was beginning to stand better, so during therapy, the therapist asked him if he wanted to look in the mirror to see himself standing. He nodded yes, and I was kind of surprised that he wanted to see himself. He did not want to before, but I thought it was too soon. I was afraid of what his reaction would be, but he did well. It was another big step for him, and I could tell that he was working as hard as he could to get better.

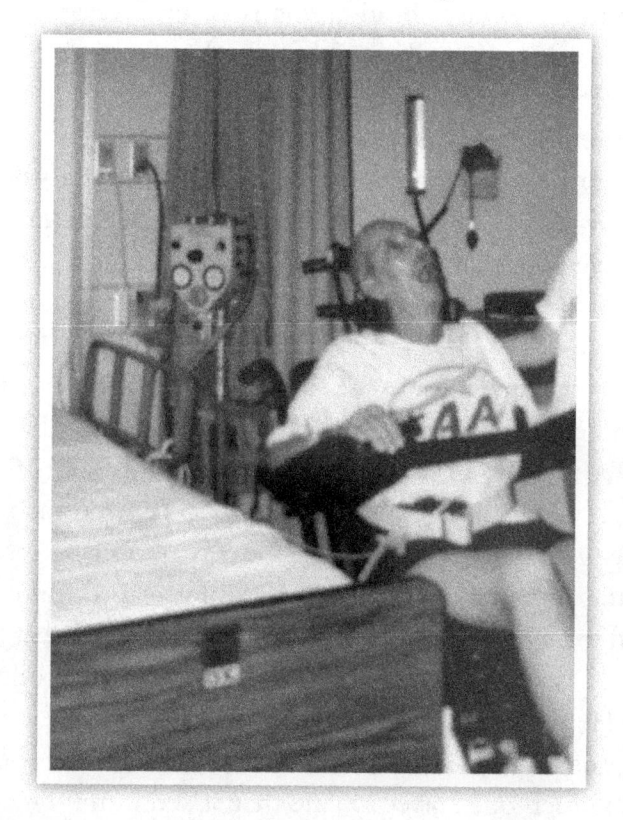

CHAPTER 9

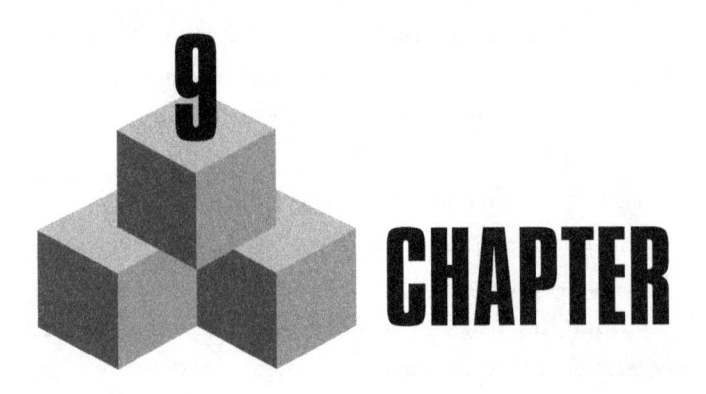

As I watched Joe day after day, working as hard as he could, I was reminded of a little plaque that I have on my desk at work. It states, "The task ahead of you is never as great as the power behind you." I thought about those words a lot, and they were so fitting for Joe.

I kept reminding myself of so many of God's promises. He said, "I am more than a conqueror." He holds victory in store for the upright. He would go before us and make our paths straight. What is impossible with men is possible with God.

It was a huge part of my life to know God, trust in God, and believe in God. So, Joe and I would just keep going.

During therapy, Joe was asked to write his name again, and he did much better. It was very small, but you could see the "Joe." He then started spelling his last name out loud. It was kind of raspy, but that didn't matter, because he was doing it. It made me remember that there were many thoughts that he may never ever speak again. He was then asked to spell my name, and it was so funny, because he started trying to spell "Doll baby," because that is what he always called me. I was laughing and asked him to spell what other people call me. He took a deep breath and spelled out each letter of my name. It was a special moment. He was asked the names of his boys, and he said each one correctly. She then asked him if he had a dog, and he nodded yes. He tried really hard to say the word *Pomeranian*, but it was too hard for him; he did, however, tell her that our dog's name was Jessie. She was sure proud of Joe that day because he tried so hard.

When we got back to Joe's room, our friends Eric and Liz were there; they began to tell us how the pottery business in our hometown was going to make a special edition piece in Joe's honor. The pieces were going to be auctioned off at the benefit auction to be held for Joe. It was so special of them to think of doing that for Joe, and I continued to be overwhelmed by the care and love that had been shown to us. Eric also brought Joe a pepper plant, which was so cool because he and Joe often got together for lunch, and most of the time, peppers would be in the meal somewhere. He also brought a crucifixion statue from Peru, which was a gift from Alfonso, the owner of Alfonso's Pizza in our hometown. Every gift was precious to us.

It was now the middle of April; it had been a month and a half since the accident, and Joe was surprising everybody with what he was able to do now. I was reminded of Genesis 28:15: "I am with you and will watch over you wherever you go. I will bring you back to this land, I will not leave you until I have done what I have promised you."

It was a tough decision to make, but it was time for me and the boys to move out of the hotel near the hospital. It was wonderful to be so close to him, but Joe was doing so much better and would hopefully be getting out before too long. We were not sure where he would be going, but I knew that I just couldn't think about moving back home yet, not without Joe.

Mark and Denise had graciously invited us to stay at their home so we could be closer to the hospital. That was an amazing offer and turned out to be a wonderful blessing to all of us. I just didn't know how I was going to handle this change in our lives, but I needed to remember that I could do all things through Christ, Who gives me strength. He had given me strength that I never had before, and with His strength, I had made it this far, and I would make it even farther.

Joe was doing better communicating. He was trying to talk more, and of course shaking hands and even trying to laugh. Laughing was something he had not done for a long, long time. When we would ask him a question, he would try to say yes or no, but then he decided to do the okay sign with his fingers. On this day, a friend of ours came to visit, and he and Joe were talking about how much they liked to box when they were younger; just then, Joe pulled at his undershorts because they were Joe Boxer brand. I didn't know that he knew that, but it was hilarious.

Just as our friend was leaving, I was interrupted by a phone call; Joe gave me a look as if to say, "Hey, you; he's leaving." It was like he was wanting me to pay attention. Once again, it was so much like Joe.

The next morning, the boys and I walked into Joe's room, and he was listening to a Christian CD by Carman. Brian had brought the CD to the hospital because we all love Carman. Our favorite song on the CD was "The Champion," and Tony turned to Joe and said, "Dad, you really put it on old Satan, didn't you?"

Joe put his fist up in the air, as if to say that he was a champion too. It brought tears to my eyes, but happiness too.

Back to therapy today, and it was a great day. The speech therapist asked Joe to tell her what doesn't belong in each group, such as peach, orange, apple, and celery. Then pie, cake, pudding, and meatloaf. He gave the correct answer each time. She was working so hard with Joe's mouth and tongue. She gave him some lemon pudding too, but he couldn't handle it well.

He was also walking better and doing more leg exercises. The therapist told us that the muscles in his legs seemed to be working correctly, which was wonderful. They wanted to see if Joe could put his shoes on and tie them. He couldn't get one of them on all the way, so he put his foot down on the floor to push his foot in. We couldn't believe he thought of that. With the other shoe, he put his leg up over his knee and then got his shoe to put it on his foot. She was so surprised that his mind helped him think to do his shoes like that. So then she decided to see if Joe could tie his shoe, and when he did, the therapist was shocked. He even tied a double tie on one of them. She clapped because she was so proud of him.

She wanted to see what else he could do, so she asked him if he could take his shirt off and put it back on. It took him awhile, but he did it. He then made fists with both of his hands to show us that he proved he could do it. She then asked Joe to sit up straight, which he was having a hard time doing. I was sitting on the floor in front of him, so I told him if he would try to do it, then I would too. He then stuck out his hand toward me to shake on it. We just made a deal! He then moved closer to me and put both hands on my face and pulled me toward him and kissed me on my cheek, and when he did, he drooled on my face. He took his rag that he used all of time, because he cannot always hold his mouth shut, and wiped my face off. I was crying by this time. It was a great day of therapy.

When we went to speech therapy, the therapist gave him a sucker and tried to get him to move it back and forth in his mouth to strengthen his tongue. She wanted him to try to blow bubbles with bubble solution; he tried hard but didn't accomplish much, even though it did make us smile. She would have him try another day.

When he got back to his room, he was tired and took a nap, and when he woke up, he kept pulling at his shirt as if he wanted to take it off. I asked him if something was wrong, and I thought I heard him say, "It's wet." I went to get the nurse, and when she came in, she said they were going to let Joe take a shower.

When he heard the nurse say that he could take a shower, he made a fist with both hands and lifted his arms. He was so excited, and so was I because it had been so long since he had taken a shower; he rested so good that night, and it was because he got to take a shower.

The next day, Joe worked so hard in therapy. The physical therapist wanted Joe to try to walk without the bars. She was on one side of him and a helper was on the other side, and he did really good. They had him roll himself over to his stomach without any help, and he was also able to prop himself up on his elbows. They also worked hard trying to get Joe to sit up straight.

He did it perfectly, and I said, "Well, look at that."

He also tried to sit back on his legs like he was kneeling, but it was too hard for him. It probably seems a little strange for me to tell you these things, but Joe had lost all control of his body. It sounds like something easy for us to do, but not for him.

When Joe went to speech therapy, the therapist worked with him to speak more instead of nodding yes or no. She gave him a mirror so he could watch his mouth move. She also said it was time to use a solution to help dry up the extra saliva, because he still had a hard time controlling it. She said that she would discuss this with his doctor to see if something else could be done to help him. She also asked Joe several questions about himself; he was able to say his name and the name of the town where he lived. He did so good. After listening to him on this day, I believed that Joe would be speaking clearly one day.

He was tired after so much therapy, and when we got back to his room, he was moving around a lot in his wheelchair. Using his right foot, he began to push his left shoe off, and then he used his left foot to push his right shoe off. I realized he was letting me know he wanted to go to bed. While he was getting into bed, the nurse came in; while she was helping him, she asked him what he wanted to do when he got home.

He said, "Everything right," and that sure brought tears to my eyes. He was super active before the accident and now had to work so hard to do every little thing.

The next day during therapy, Joe had trouble with depth perception. He seemed to reach way past an item. The therapist was using colored clothespins and a yardstick, and Joe could not seem to latch the pins on the yardstick. She then used a tabletop ladder and asked him to put the pegs in holes on the ladder, and he did do better.

The speech therapist was also pleased with Joe. He was able to say his name and his hometown again. She told him that she was from Indiana, and Joe spoke up and said, "I will pray for you." It was so funny; we couldn't help but laugh. She asked him more questions about our sons, and he answered everything perfectly. She knew that he was giving the correct answer because she had the information in front of her.

When it was time to go back to his room, Joe told me that he wanted to go home. We had not talked about this, and it's hard to write about this because it brought tears to my eyes then, and it brings tears to my eyes now. We had been through so much together, and he had worked so very, very hard to get to where he was now. I know he had to be tired, but he still had a lot of hard work to do. I tried not to fall apart and told him that there was more that he'd need to do before we could leave. I then told him that we needed to be able to use the gym and equipment that was there for him to become stronger, and I told him not to worry about things at home, because the bills were being paid, and everything was okay.

I didn't say this to Joe, but after the accident happened, I didn't know if he would ever be where he was now. It was only because of God and His love for us that we got this far.

Joe fell right to sleep. I sat there for hours, it seemed, just looking at him and praying.

Our case worker came in the next morning to give us a report. She said she always looked forward to going to the meetings about Joe, because of all the good news that she heard about him. Everyone said how amazing it was that Joe could do what he does, considering how bad the head injury was. They had set a day for his discharge: May 14, but I was not sure where he would be going for more therapy, and his doctor wanted Joe to have another week of therapy here.

It was another day, and since we were still at this hospital, we went off to therapy again. They wanted to see if Joe could do better walking. One of the helpers sat on a stool with wheels on it in front of Joe to make sure as he walked, he was able to keep his feet a good distance apart. He needed to be able to keep his balance too, and he did better than expected.

When he finished with therapy, we went back to his room, where he had a lot of company. So many of our family came over; they did not get to visit for very long, but they were so happy to see how well Joe was doing. Willie, a close friend, walked in, and he and Joe started talking, as best Joe could, and all of a sudden, Joe said, "Okay, Willie." Just as clearly as if you or I were saying it. That put a smile on everybody's face. It was so great to see everyone, and Joe had a great time.

It was now April 22, and so much of Joe's character had been showing up; some of the little things that he used to say appeared at different times. Once again, I was reminded that God sometimes shows up suddenly, and when I came into Joe's room that day, one of the doctors was talking to him about our family picture, which had moved with him all along the way. She asked us if we had any questions because she was trying to explain head injuries and memory and other functions. I knew that I had some questions within me somewhere, but I was just overwhelmed. She said that she wanted to put Joe through a full day of intense testing during the next week. I knew they needed to make sure he was ready to be discharged.

I told her about the importance of God in our lives and said how I believed that God had really shown up for Joe and how all his steps have been ordered by God. She told me she believed that too. I told her they called Joe the "Miracle Man" at the hospital in Springfield and how excited everyone was for him; it was a miracle that he even survived the injury. She told me that everyone there was talking about Joe and his progress, and people were surprised that he could do what he could do because of the injury.

When we went to physical therapy, Joe was able to move his left leg and left foot all at the same time. Everyone there was clapping for him. In speech therapy, he was able to say many more names and words. I knew this was one of those times when God had moved suddenly, and I had my eyes wide open to what God was doing. Since the day Joe told me he wanted to go home, there had been a noticeable change in what he could do.

They asked him how many years we had been married, and he answered, "All my life"; then he said, correctly, "Twenty-eight years." He was now able to say the ABCs and counted to five. The therapist wanted him to try to make sounds such as mmmmm, ta ta ta, and pa pa pa, and he did really good. When we were leaving therapy, he looked around and told her goodbye.

I saw her take a quick glance back at him as if to say, "Did he say that?"

I nodded yes. He was trying to talk up a storm.

When we were back in his room, the phone rang; I put it up to his ear, and he just kept talking. It was so much like Joe that it brought tears to my eyes. When he was done talking, he handed the phone to me; it was a really good friend of ours, so I asked him if he could understand Joe, and he said he was surprisingly shocked because he could understand him so well.

Joe had more therapy later in the day; he was working with the arm cycle and seemed to have a hard time focusing; when he grabbed the handles, he seemed to grab past the handles. As the therapist was watching him, she noticed his difficulty, so decided to put a patch over one eye and then over the other eye. When the patch was put over the right eye, he was able to focus better, and when the patch was over the left eye, it helped even more. So, it looked like he would wear a patch for a while.

After Joe finished with therapy, I asked him if he wanted to go outside on the patio. I couldn't understand his answer, so I asked him again, and he said, "I don't care if you want to."

I just looked at him for a minute, and we headed outside, but we didn't stay long because he was tired. We went back to his room, and he wanted to lay down. He fell asleep, and I noticed how restless he seemed. I had not noticed him being that restless before. I decided to go ahead and leave so he could rest. I called around ten o'clock to see how he was doing, and they told me he was coughing a lot, so they rolled him over to his side. I was also told that the more alert he became, the more restless and anxious he could become. It was all due to the head injury.

Tomorrow was another day, and God did more amazing things in Joe.

4-24-99

Joe Lakin

CHAPTER 10

The next day, bright and early, Joe was going to physical therapy. He walked farther that day by himself than he ever had. The floor there had a design of blocks in it, and on this day, Joe looked at me and asked me how many blocks he had walked, and I told him it was forty-two blocks. He then told me that he was going to go farther the next time. I could tell that he was so happy.

The speech therapist wanted to try something new for Joe. If you will remember, he could not close his mouth, control his tongue, or even hold saliva in his mouth. It just ran out of his mouth. Well, today she wanted to see if Joe could try to eat some applesauce; I watched and wondered if he could do it, but he couldn't get it to go back into his throat to swallow it. It sounds easy, but it wasn't easy for Joe.

When Joe was in occupational therapy, he tried to lay on his belly and then get up on his knees to rock back and forth. He tried to move backward on his knees and then forward like he was crawling. He couldn't do that very long, but he did do it. Joe then told the therapist that he wanted to sit in a regular chair; his request surprised her, but she thought it would be okay as long as someone was with him; she was excited that he wanted to try something different. Before he was done for the day, she had him place shapes in the right spaces, and he did it in record time. She also had him move shower curtain rings across an arch that was made of a hula hoop; he used both hands to do it, which was different for him. He had a small smile on his face, which was good to see.

When we got back to Joe's room, his doctor came in and told us that he had recovered from his head injury faster than anyone she had ever seen. I looked over at Joe and thought to myself, *He had what she called a "quick" recovery because God was in control of every step he had taken.*

When Joe went to speech therapy the next day, he was so much like his old self that I had to leave the room. It was so emotional for me, and I didn't want him to see me crying. After I pulled myself back together, I went back into the room, and Joe was reading complete sentences. I think I was in shock, and as he was reading, some friends of ours came into the room. Joe looked at them and introduced them to the therapist, saying their names perfectly. He saw some bubble solution sitting on the table and wanted to blow bubbles, which he was not able to do previously. We didn't know if he could really do that now, but he did, and we all laughed so hard. It had been a long time since we'd heard him laugh, and it felt so good.

As we were going back to his room, he again told me he wanted to go home. I told him that we had not been released to leave yet, and then he told me he wanted to go to Carrollton. Tears began to fill my eyes because I knew he was missing home; so was I.

After his nap, he wanted to sit in a regular chair and asked to see the cards that had been sent to him. He told me that he wanted to read them himself, so I held them for him, and he did so good reading them. As he read each card, we would talk more about them, and he did so good having a conversation. As we were looking at the cards, some of our friends came into the room; Joe was especially glad to see them, and we all had a conversation. He was so much like himself that I just kept looking at him. One of our friends said there was something different about Joe's room; she said she could feel something different there. She added that she could feel so much love between Joe and I in the room; I was thrilled to hear her say that. There had been so many changes in Joe that I was glad that others could feel the love he and I still had for each other. After everyone left, Joe again said that he wanted to go home. Going home was on his mind a lot now. I told him that I would not go home and stay there without him. God knew the desires of Joe's heart. Psalm 20:4 states, "May he give you the desire of your heart and make all your plans succeed."

Later in the day, his doctor came in to see him again; this time, she checked his peripheral vision. He was having trouble, especially in the left eye, but she told us that his vision was perfect. That was remarkable. She said she needed to tell us again that Joe is the quickest recovery she has ever witnessed. One of his nurses came in while the doctor was still there and told us that she had worked in the brain injury unit for twenty-five years; she said that Joe was doing tremendous and showed so much potential. There was not a doubt in my mind that God had never left our side.

We don't know why God chose this path for us to walk, but He did. It was not for our purpose but for His. I was reminded every day that God is the power inside us and all around us, the presence beside us and the purpose before us. We could not be doing this walk without Him with us. I knew that God had a plan for all of this, but we couldn't see what it was right now; at times, I felt so unworthy to do what God had called us to do. In the Bible, many of those God chose felt like they were unworthy, but one thing I am sure of is that all of this was for his glory.

So we would keep taking one step at a time and working hard.

The next day in speech therapy, the therapist wanted to try to stimulate Joe's mouth, so she wanted him to suck on lemon glycerin swabs as much as possible. Not something I would want to do. She also tried papaya juice and meat tenderizer. She put some sugar on a mouth swab to see if Joe could taste it, but he couldn't, and she told me that it would be important to use a toothbrush for stimulation on his tongue and especially on the back of his tongue. Joe had lost all control of his mouth and throat muscles; his mouth just fell open all the time, and he couldn't hold his saliva, but the therapist was trying to help him regain control.

That day at occupational therapy, Joe was asked to stack plastic cones on each other, place a stick up and down on the table ladder, and play catch with a balloon. I know this sounds simple to us, but it was not for Joe. He also seemed to tire easily, so we went back to his room, but when we got there, he wanted to look at more of the cards that had been sent to him; he really enjoyed seeing how people were thinking of him. It didn't last long, though, because he decided he wanted to try to get into the bed by himself, and he did pretty good.

When I came into his room the next day, he said again that he wanted to go home. I felt so sorry for him; we talked about why he had to stay longer, and it seemed to help relax him. He was able to get into his chair with my help, and he tried several times to get up out of it by himself. He seemed to want to try to do more by himself, so I handed him a pencil and paper and asked him to write his name. He really tried hard but needed more practice.

When we got to physical therapy, a man we had never met before was there. Joe motioned for me to go over to the man; he wanted to know what happened to Joe, so I told him about the accident. He began to cry and told me that it broke his heart. He told us that he didn't know if he was going to get back to 100 percent, either, but he was sure trying; he was only there for therapy for his leg. I told him not to give up; we prayed for him and told him we would continue to ask God to help him.

When we got back to Joe's room, the nurse brought a TV and a VCR and some movies. He picked a John Wayne movie, and then she said, "Well, Mr. Expert, show me how you can get into bed by yourself."

He did it without any help, and then we watched the movie together. It was a nice quiet night.

I needed to go back to our house the next day to take care of some things, but I didn't want to leave Joe alone, so Toni offered to stay with him, then I felt better about going. I found out when I got back that Joe had walked almost the whole length of the therapy room. Yay! I was also told that in speech therapy, he was asked some questions, such as the year, three things that he did that morning, and who was with him, and he did good. It didn't take much for Joe to get tired, so the therapist got a cold rag to put on his face, and that made him more alert, so she was able to work with him a little longer. She had asked Joe to try to fill his cheeks up with air and move the air from side to side in his mouth; it was sure hard for him, but he kept trying. She also wanted Joe to try to say the "K" letter better, so he kept trying and trying.

When Joe got to occupational therapy, the therapist asked how his weekend was, and he said, "Boring," which wasn't what she expected to hear. She asked him to hold his arms out straight in front of him; first the left arm and then the right arm. She then had him straighten his fingers out while he was holding his arms up in the air. That was something different for him too.

Then Toni said, "Joe, praise the Lord," and he raised his arms straight up and stretched his fingers out real straight. When Toni told me that, I was so proud because Joe truly loves the Lord with all his heart.

Joe continued to walk farther each day, and he stopped sliding his feet so much. He was learning how to pick his foot up with each step. With every new step that Joe would take, it was another step closer to going home. You know what else was really exciting that day? I only had to wipe saliva off his face twice.

Joe used to be able to do anything and everything, so watching him do this therapy was truly emotional. Sometimes, we are heading down a path that we did not choose, but it is during those times that we know God is with us and will never leave us. I watched Joe use an arm skate to go back and forth on a table, take shapes off a board with his left hand and put them back on with his right hand, and use an arm pulley to strengthen his arms. He had to work so hard to do these simple things.

When we got to speech therapy, the therapist was not there. Joe looked around everywhere but did not see her. He then told me, "I'm here and I am ready."

I looked at him and shrugged my shoulders.

When she did arrive, Joe told her that he was ready. She smiled at him and then asked him to try to read some sentences; she wanted to hear more of the "ah," "oh," and "ee" sounds. Right in the middle of the sentences, Joe stopped and asked her where her glasses were because she did not have them on. You should have seen the surprised look on her face. She could not believe that he noticed something like that; it was certainly unexpected, and she loved it. She then said that she wanted him to continue doing sentences, but no longer than fifteen minutes at a time.

After we went back to his room, we did some more reading, but just a little. He put his house slippers on by himself and then looked up and saw a friend of ours who had come in; Joe told him he needed a haircut and that he'd be glad to do it for him. It was so funny because Joe still had a black patch over one eye, but he had noticed our friend's hair and made a comment about it.

He wanted to play cards with our friends, so we agreed and ended up playing three games; Joe won all three games. He even shuffled the cards and dealt them correctly. We all just looked at him and each other as if to say, "Did we just watch him do that?"

He told me that he was thirsty and wanted a drink from the drinking fountain, which he had not been able to do, because he could not control the fluid once it was in his mouth. I took him to get a drink, and we were both surprised how well he did; he said he really liked the water.

I think I was in shock because of everything he was able to do that day.

CHAPTER 11

Joe's head injury happened on March 1; it was now April 27. So much had happened.

That morning, I received a call from the hospital at 6:45. Joe had fallen out of bed. I had a lot of questions about how that could happen. Brian and I were on our way. After we arrived, Joe told us that he tried to get out of the bed to empty the commode sitting next to his bed. His doctor came in and explained that she would have an alarm put on his bed. She told us Joe was past needing bed restraints, but as he became more active, his brain was starting to make decisions, and mistakes like this were part of the brain injury healing itself. That was something totally new for him. And for me.

He had another vigorous day of therapy. Something totally different happened that day, which was something I seemed to be saying a lot. The speech therapist asked Joe about the weather outside, and Joe used a cuss word when he replied. She couldn't believe he said that word, so she asked him again, and he said it again. She was shocked, and I was too; I couldn't fight the tears off. This was something new that his brain was telling him, but it wasn't easy to accept. Before the accident, if someone cussed when we were around other people, he never did like it and would always say, "Please don't talk like that; there is a lady present here." I guess I would need to be more mindful that situations like this could happen.

The therapist continued with therapy; she put grapefruit juice on a mouth swab to time his swallowing; his time was 12.3 seconds, and 2.3 was normal swallowing time. Then she read some stories to Joe and asked him questions to see what he could remember. He answered eight of nine questions correct about the first story and six of seven correct about the second story. She said his short-term memory ability was great, but he was tired when he finished, so he went to his room to take a nap.

As he was waking up, a therapy dog came into his room. I wasn't sure how he was going to react because he did not care for dogs, but he enjoyed playing with the dog and actually laughed out loud. He seemed to be surprising me a lot lately. This was the first time in a very long time that I had heard Joe laugh out loud. It was so nice to hear.

Later in the day, Pastor Sam came to visit, and while he was there, he laid hands on Joe and then on me, and when Joe saw that Pastor had laid his hands on him, then Joe put his hand on me to pray too. When the prayer was over, Joe said, "Amen," and that really seemed like old times.

The next day, another blessing was brought to us. Two of the ladies that I worked with came to see us; one of them was my supervisor. They brought a card from the people at the dental school, and inside was a check from a man who brought the check to the school after hearing about me and Joe. He just felt the need to do something for us. That was a wonderful blessing, and I just knew that God would bless him for blessing us. That is just how the Lord works.

By the end of April, so much had happened. I was reminded of Isaiah 43:18, which says, "Forget the former things, do not dwell on the past. See, I am doing a new thing. Now, it springs up, do you not perceive it? I am making a way in the desert and streams in the wasteland." This scripture would help me to keep looking forward because God was doing a new thing. He was not finished yet. There was so much more to come.

Things were happening quickly. In physical therapy, Joe walked faster and farther than he ever had. He even walked into the hallway; his therapist told me he no longer needed his special chair. She went to get a different chair for him, and he was able to back this chair up with his feet. She put his right leg on the footrest to make his left leg work harder. That leg needs to become stronger, so this was a way to help him make that happen.

During physical therapy, he was asked to take his shirt off and try to put it back on by himself; to our surprise, he could do it. He was also able to put clothespins on a stick and could take his shoes off by himself and put them back on too. Have you ever thought of not being able to take your shirt off or not being able to put your shoes on? It reminded me that we take so much for granted.

His therapists and I discussed how he was able to do so much, including doing several things at a time; we could tell that he was trying to make more decisions on his own, which meant that his brain was waking up.

When we got back to his room, his doctor came in and asked if I knew anything about a redness on the right side of Joe's face. She said she didn't believe it was caused by falling out of bed. I told her about how the right side of his face had been damaged by the accident, thinking that might be causing the redness. I knew it was in his files from the previous hospital; before we left the hospital in Springfield, his doctor wanted to rescan that area in six weeks, but we left before it was done. She was glad I knew what was going on, so she decided to call in another doctor to check his face. Before she left his room, she told me she thought Joe was phenomenal, and she had been so encouraged by him; she looked over at Joe and told him to keep up the good work.

After his doctor left, Lisa, our insurance representative, came in with some good news for us. She said they would consider releasing Joe if we had a place to stay in Alton; Joe would need to continue extensive therapy, and our home was quite a distance from the hospital. How exciting was that? In the back of my mind, I recalled that Mark and Denise offered their home to us for a place to stay, which was truly a blessing. Needless to say, Joe had a huge smile on his face as he listened to the doctor.

After all this wonderful news, Joe went to therapy; just outside the therapy room, we saw a lady coming toward us, so we stopped. She took his hands and began praying for him. We didn't even know who she was and had never seen her in the hospital before. It was just like God to place his angels all around us, right now, and right in this place. When she was done praying, she hugged me and walked away. I had no time to speak to her before she walked away, and we never did see her again. I smiled because I knew that God places his angels everywhere.

Joe did great in therapy, and as I watched him, I was reminded of when he took his first steps in this room.

Later that evening, when we were back in Joe's room, we decided to play a game; just as we were beginning, the phone rang. Joe answered it, which surprised me; he looked over and then handed me the phone. I talked for just a bit, and then he motioned for me and gave me this look of "Are you going to talk on the phone or play the game?"

I started laughing so hard that I think I was crying at the same time. After we finished playing the game, we decided to open some of his mail. I noticed an envelope that I didn't recognize the return address on, and when I opened it, the card inside read, "Praying for you every day," and signed "a friend always." The card had a twenty-dollar bill in it. We didn't have a clue who this came from, and we never found out, but we praised the Lord and prayed together that this person would truly be blessed.

The next day, Joe had a new CT scan of his head. His doctor came in with the report and told us she couldn't ask for anything better, considering how bad the injury was. We found out that his brain was healing well, and a lot of the bleeding had dried up. This was really good news; so many things began to happen that day. After his doctor left his room, a psychologist came in to ask Joe some questions. I was told that I could stay in the room but couldn't help him answer. I wasn't sure how he would do, and she didn't tell us her decision. I was sure that we would find out, sometime.

I could tell that the news was out that Joe would be leaving soon. One of the sisters from the hospital came in to talk to me about

Joe's accident. It was hard to relive everything that had happened; it seemed as if it happened just yesterday. She was so touched and so understanding, and she even had tears in her eyes. She then asked me if it would be okay if she could write an article about Joe so others would be blessed by his story. She also wanted to know if I would speak to someone from a St. Louis newspaper and maybe a TV station. I, of course, agreed. I wanted to share Joe's story as much as I could about safety when working and especially when trimming trees, but most of all about belief and faith in God.

While all of this had been going on, therapy continued. He was walking twice a day now; he would stand in front of a mirror and try to kick his legs from side to side and to step from side to side. This was to help him with his feet placement when he walked. It made me stop and think about how hard Joe had to work to make sure his feet were in the correct place before walking. He was also able to get up from the mat to the table by himself and roll over on his belly, get up on his hands and knees, and crawl forward and back. I remembered when he was just learning to do these things. Tears came to my eyes when I saw him start to fall and I couldn't help him; that was so hard for me. I wanted to help him, but I had to remember that he needed to learn to help himself.

He did something different in speech therapy that day too. The therapist read some sentences to him, and then he tried to read them and also do what the sentences told him to do. He had never been able to do that, but it was so encouraging to watch him. The more he was able to do, the more I realized that his brain was waking up even more.

He was tired, and I couldn't blame him because the therapists were working him so hard. On the way back to his room, he told me he wanted to go home, and he wanted to go out to eat. When we got to his room, he found a piece of paper and tried to write a note. It took him a little bit of time, but it said, "we went to supper." I started crying and explained to him that we couldn't leave just yet but hopefully soon.

He got upset with me because we couldn't leave, and he even

said some things that really hurt my feelings. It was very emotional for me; I had never seen Joe react like that. It was a part of the brain injury that I had not dealt with yet, but I knew that it could happen. I didn't let him know how much it hurt me but explained that he needed to be able to swallow better before we could go out to eat; then I surprised him by saying it was possible that we could be leaving there in two weeks. I could tell that the news of leaving made his mood change for the better.

It was now the end of April; hard to believe another month had gone by. Joe was still working extremely hard to get better; he wanted to be able to leave. He was walking farther and even walked out to the patio, which was quite a bit of a distance. You know what else was great about this walk? It was the first time he walked with just the therapist; I didn't have to follow him with the wheelchair, and he even made it that far without having to sit down. It was so great to see him try to accomplish something new every day. Sometimes, when he tried to do something, it seemed to us like it was in slow motion, but when he would do it, we would be so happy for him.

When we came back in from the patio, we moved on to speech therapy; he tried to drink cranberry juice through a straw, but he couldn't swallow it, so he tried with a spoon; he took too much, and that made him choke. His swallowing muscles still needed a lot of work.

You know, as I watched Joe every day, I couldn't help but wonder what he was thinking. I mean, did he realize what happened to him and why he was having to do all this?

The first day of May was an unexpected, blessed day for sure. This was how it all started: I received a call asking if I could meet someone at our house. I made arrangements to leave for a while, and Tony and I drove up to our house, not having any idea what to expect. When we got there, Connie, our friend Denise's sister, and the owner of a construction company were there. He wanted to see what needed to be done to finish our house.

We were shocked and didn't really know what was going on. You see, when Denise heard about Joe's accident, she immediately started praying and was feeling like God was laying a burden on her for our family. She wasn't sure what it was all about and asked her husband and mom to pray with her to get an answer from God. The answer did come, and God showed her that because of the accident, He wanted to move through other people to be a blessing for us and to receive blessings from God in their own lives.

That's why we were called to come to our house. The house still had a lot to be done. Joe and I would work on it whenever we had a little bit of extra money; we were determined not to borrow money to get it done. I hadn't even thought about the house not being done since Joe's accident, but now that I did, I realized that we could not finish it (I wasn't sure what abilities Joe would have).

The construction worker walked through the house and made a list of the major projects yet to be done. Tears came to my eyes as I looked through the house because it made me feel like nothing would ever be the same; everything had changed for us, but you know what? This was still our home; it had always been filled with hard work and lots of love.

In the midst of everything that was going on, I found out that I would be going back to work in early May, and we had a place to stay in Alton. Denise and Mark once again invited us to stay at their home. They moved out of their bedroom and into another bedroom in their house so when Joe got out of the hospital, we would be close to the bathroom and the kitchen. I didn't know how I would ever thank them.

I went to work in the morning and then went to the hospital at noon. It was going to be hard not being at the hospital with Joe all the time. I hoped I could do this, but I knew that it was just another step for us to take.

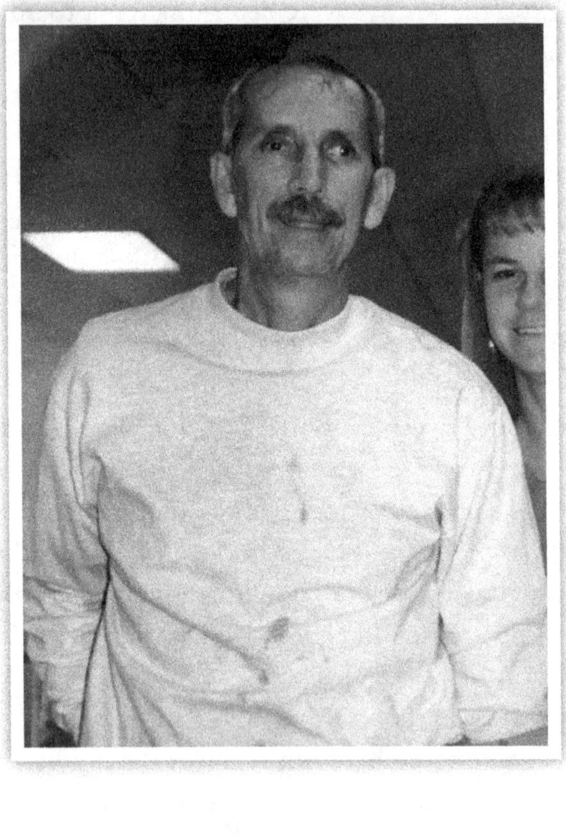

CHAPTER 12

On May 3, I worked that morning and finally got to the hospital to be with Joe. I was told that he worked super hard that morning and tried to shave himself; he did pretty good but when I got there, he asked me to "touch it up just a little." We also went to the gift shop, which was a first for us, because he wanted to pick out a card for his mother for Mother's Day. He told me that he thought about doing this by himself, which would have been a huge undertaking and a huge surprise. He did really good looking at the cards, and I could tell that he enjoyed it because he was doing something for someone else.

When we got back to his room, his speech therapist told us that she wanted Joe to work on whistling, smiling, and growling. I had a feeling that this was going to be funny for both of us. She did some mouth exercises with him and said that she was stumped by his lack of mouth control, suggesting it could be a nerve problem. If so, it could take longer to work out.

So a new CT scan was taken, and his doctor said she was very happy; it showed that the bone was healing over the separation in the back of his sinuses. She was also impressed because he was going to the bathroom by himself and shaving himself; she said that "he was sure determined."

Brian was in the room with us, and she heard Joe tell him if he was tired, he could lay down next to him and take a nap, but he might kick him out of the bed; then he laughed and gave Brian a big fist with his right hand. Even the doctor laughed over that one.

It was storming bad when it was time for us to leave, and Joe was worried about us driving in the bad weather. I told him we would be all right until we got back to Mark and Denise's. He seemed more relieved then, but I asked him if he was going to be okay in the storm, and he nodded his head yes. It was so sweet of him to be concerned about us. I didn't want him to worry, though.

Joe's sister, Barbie, who was a nurse, called me the next day to check on us; she was concerned about the difficulty he still had in swallowing. She asked if I remembered that right after the accident, they tried three times to intubate him; he fought them hard and even pulled the tube back out. She said that it could definitely cause trauma to his tongue and mouth.

I remember how swollen and black and blue his face and tongue were shortly after the accident. There were times when I wondered if Joe pulled the tube out of his throat to tell them he did not want to be kept alive. At that time, I was told that he needed to be intubated to help him breathe; they wanted him to breathe easier because the cranial pressure was so dangerously high.

Joe seemed to be doing so well in physical and occupational therapy, but he still had trouble concentrating in speech therapy; his therapist was determined to figure out what was happening. She was trying to build up his esophagus and the muscles in his neck. She tried applesauce, but he could only swallow a quarter of a teaspoon.

His voice sounded rough, so she knew that some applesauce went down the wrong way, but he didn't cough or gag, so she knew that the message wasn't letting him know it went down the wrong way. She said they would do neuro testing next week, and I was so thankful that she could now tell what was happening.

After he was done with speech, we received more great news: Joe no longer needed breathing treatments. It had been part of his daily routine for so long that this was awesome news.

When we got back to his room, Joe needed to go to the bathroom; our favorite nurse's aide was in his room, and she wanted to show me how to transfer Joe from one area to another. I would need to know how to do this before he could leave. She was just an adorable person, and as we were transferring Joe, she said that she loved us so much and could not believe how far Joe had come. She believed that he had truly been touched by God, and she had never seen someone do what he had. She told me that when she read his reports that came with him to this hospital, she could not believe that he was still alive. At the time of the accident, fluid from Joe's brain was coming down into his mouth; it caused a cough for a long time but would eventually go away. She said that sometimes our bodies need to get caught back up with our brain.

As she and I talked, I received a call asking if I'd be there in the evening because a reporter from Channel 5 wanted to come by and talk to us. He showed up around five o'clock and interviewed me and Joe. Joe was sitting up in his bed, and I sat next to his bed. I was asked about the accident and where we were now. He asked Joe if he could walk a little out in the hall for him, and with the help of our favorite nurse's aide, he did really good, even with a patch over one eye. The reporter also spoke to Joe's doctor, who described his injury and therapy. He took a family picture and told us that we would be on the news that evening. I, of course, called all our family and friends to let them know we would be on the news that night. It was a big night for Joe, and I could tell he was tired, so I helped him get into bed. After he fell asleep, I left for the night.

The next morning, Tony and I went back to the hospital. As soon as we went into Joe's room, I walked over to his bed; he pulled my face down toward his and asked me to take him home. It just broke my heart; I had to tell him that we needed a little more time before he was ready to go home. I also told him there were some things that the boys and I needed to be trained to do, but hopefully, it wouldn't be too long.

In therapy, he was asked to fold some towels and unscrew and screw nuts and bolts on a board. He was also able to take plastic pegs off a board and put them in a container. He seemed to really enjoy doing this one, because he kept doing it over and over.

In speech therapy, he was asked to read some sentences, and I couldn't believe how well he did. While I was sitting there and watching him, my thoughts were taken back to how bad the accident was; seeing him do this now was such a blessing.

Just then, his doctor walked in, and she said, "Joe can have a day pass to go home tomorrow."

Did I just hear her say that Joe could go home for a day? The boys and I quickly learned how to get Joe in and out of a car, but when we tried it with him, he did it pretty much all by himself. The therapist was impressed and even clapped her hands. Next, they explained the feeding tube process, but I had watched it so many times that I was able to do it by myself. We were willing to do whatever it took to help Joe go home.

On the way home that evening, Tony and I talked about how much had happened to our family in the past five years. The more we talked about it, the more we could visualize the hands of God leading the way. We had been through some tough times and sometimes wondered if we were going to make it through. It was hard to see the good through the bad, but no matter what, God did not leave us or forsake us. His Word tells us that there will be tough times, but He will be with us, and we won't have to walk through them alone. He will carry us when He needs to.

You may have read the story of a man who dreamed he was walking on the beach with Jesus; he looked back and saw two sets of footprints, where they walked together, but then he saw a troubled time in his life, and there was only one set of footprints. Jesus told him during those times, He was carrying him. Deuteronomy 1:31 says; "There you saw how the Lord your God carried you, as a father carries is son, all the way you went until you reached this place." This place was where we were right now.

May 9 was on Mother's Day weekend, and Joe was coming back home to Carrollton. The boys and I got to the hospital around eight o'clock, and he was ready to go. He truly enjoyed the ride. It had been a long time since he had been in a car. When we got to the house, he needed help getting up the five steps to the back porch, but Tony and Brian helped him. He walked slowly into the house and just looked at everything, like everything was new to him; he was concentrating so hard. It was like he was trying to figure some things out. We had a lot of visitors come by to see him, and it was a great day. When it came time for him to go back, he didn't seem upset, but I could tell he was worn out. It was a lot for him in one day. I was proud of him for doing so well.

The next day, he did exceptionally good in physical and occupational therapy. His therapist talked to us about improving his concentration and explained that it was typical with brain injuries. He then told us that he could tell how hard it was to concentrate.

His speech therapist noticed that his control seemed worse. She decided to try pineapple juice to see if it would help, and it did; she was surprised it worked so well. She asked him what foods he would like to eat. She named several foods to try and see what his brain could be telling him, and he chose lime Jell-O and mashed potatoes. She told him she'd speak to his doctor about a medication to dry up the saliva. Hopefully, we would find out about that tomorrow.

I decided to go and get lunch while Joe rested; when I got back, I was told that he got himself up out of bed to go to the bathroom. When I asked about it, the nurse's aide told me that when he came into Joe's room, he was out of his bed, and the bathroom door was shut. He had walked from the bed to the bathroom by himself. It made me wonder what he would try to do by himself next.

We went to physical therapy later, and he did really well. He was asked to walk on a certain type of mat to practice walking on carpet or grass. That was sure different for him, but he didn't have any difficulty walking on it. In speech therapy, he was given some Jell-O to use for the first time for cough reflex. The therapist was truly excited because her ideas were beginning to work for him.

While all of this was going on, we heard that his doctor said no to the saliva medication. She didn't want to take a chance on raising his blood pressure; that would not be good. I guess something else would have to be tried, so we went back to his room.

Joe asked me to take off his shoes, but I told him he needed to do it himself. He was not very happy with me, but I explained that I had been told to encourage him to do it. The nurse's aide came in and said she wanted to show me how to help him in the shower; she said that I would also be doing his 8 p.m. feeding tube treatment. I knew they wanted to make sure that I could take care of him when we went home.

The next day, Joe had another outing to the St. Louis Art Museum. It was good for him to go on these outings; they helped him cope in the outside world. When he came back from the museum, his social worker came in to talk to us about his discharge. We were sure surprised, so when the nurse came in, I talked to her about his coughing because it was still so bad; she said there may be some paralysis in the throat, so when he lays down, the saliva drains into his throat. He would not know it was happening, and that could cause him to cough. We would see what would be decided about the cough.

Joe was sure busy the next day. He did the routine exercises in the morning, but in the afternoon, he walked, did steps in the gym and in the stairwell which was new for him. He needed to take a step at a time with both feet, instead of one foot at a time. Someone needed to stay in front of him when he went down the steps and behind him when he went up. He did better than we thought he would. It seemed like the therapists were watching him more closely; they wanted to see what he could do before being discharged.

He had a swallow test that afternoon, but the test did not show a passing code, so it would need to be done again in two weeks. We were all hoping he would pass the test. His doctor felt like Joe was nervous during the test and didn't really understand what was happening; that could have been why he didn't pass. So when he did get to leave here, he would not be able to eat food because the swallow test was not successful. Joe told the doctor he didn't think his throat was working, and the speech therapist said that she probably should not have said, "Joe, swallow; it isn't working." She said it probably made him more nervous.

His doctor told us she was going to fill out the papers for Joe to apply for disability. She said that even though he had done so well, it could be a couple of years before he could work in a salon again or to do any type of job. She said she wouldn't be surprised if it happened sooner, since he surprised everyone there, but there were no guarantees.

Then she looked at Joe and said, "No more trimming trees or construction work."

She also told us that the x-rays from the swallow test showed that his throat muscles were working; sometimes after an injury like Joe's, the mouth will just start working suddenly, but sometimes, it takes longer. No one really knows. She would send him home with the tube, food cans and medications.

That day, Joe tried to walk with a cane; he had never tried that before. He couldn't walk with it very well and did better with someone helping him. It was just too early to use a cane or walker.

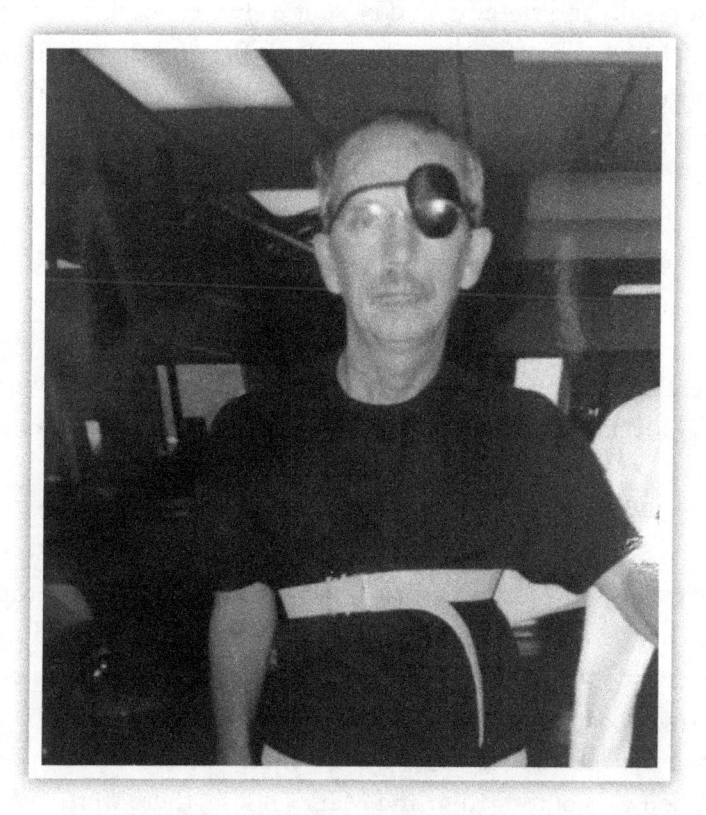

CHAPTER 13

It was May 14, and Joe was being released from the hospital. Brian went to the hospital to stay with him until I got there about one o'clock. Joe did not have therapy, and we were told that all his test results and notes would be sent to Hazelwood, an outpatient facility. I had a lot of papers to sign, and Brian gathered all of Joe's belongings. Then we went to tell his doctor and all the therapists goodbye, and that was not easy; they were like family to us and had touched our lives in a way that would never be forgotten. As I am typing this, I can feel the emotions that I felt on that day. We all had tears in our eyes.

I remember how I felt when Joe first arrived at this hospital. I thought I had made the wrong decision for him to be there, but now, he was able to move all his body parts. After a lot of hard work and with God helping him along the way, he was walking out of this hospital.

Around two o'clock, we left the hospital, and before we got very far, Joe asked me to cut off his hospital bracelets. He was so happy; I didn't want him to know that I had mixed feelings even though I was so happy too. It was going to be so different for all of us. The first thing he wanted to do was get his hair cut, so we stopped at a salon owned by our friend Gary; he was so excited to see Joe and so touched that he wanted to stop there first.

When we got to Denise and Mark's house, there were "Welcome

home" banners in the front yard, and the inside of the house was decorated too. They had given up so much for us to have a place to stay. It was wonderful and so thoughtful, and it sure put a big smile on Joe's face.

Things were about to change in a lot of different ways. Again. It was wonderful for Joe to be out of the hospital and great that I didn't have to drive there every day, but still, each day would have its challenges. It was the weekend, and a lot of people came to see how Joe was doing; someone even asked if he wanted to go play pool in the basement. He took his time going down the steps, and I was in front of him because that is what I was taught to do. He did well playing pool, but I had to stand behind him, holding onto the support that was around his waist, to help with his balance.

He was tired after a long day of visiting and didn't sleep very well that night. He coughed a lot, and there just wasn't anything I could do to help him; all I could do was keep him comfortable. I felt helpless and just started crying and got up to pray. We were used to Joe having trained professionals to help him, and now it was just us.

May 17 was another step to take; it was the first day at the new rehab center. Joe and I got there at 8:30 a.m.; I didn't know what to expect, so I was very nervous. The first thing I found out was that they weren't ready for Joe to be there. They did not have any of his feeding tube supplies so it was a good thing that before we left the house, I got a couple of cans of milk and a syringe, just in case. Good thing I did, but then I had to show the assistant how to do the treatment because she didn't know how. I didn't really feel comfortable leaving him, but relatives were not allowed to stay. I was told to pick him up at three o'clock. This was so hard, and when I got back to my car, I just cried.

When I arrived to pick Joe up, I was told that he did well. We got home in time for supper, and he told me he was hungry. I fixed some soup broth, and he surprised us and did really well. His brain seemed to be telling him when he wanted something, so we would try to wake up his taste buds. We all tried not to leave food sitting around the house, but he noticed a 3 Musketeers candy bar, which had always been his favorite. I cut off a couple tiny pieces and gave them to him (he did so well but, of course, wanted the whole candy bar).

We sat down with Mark and Denise to make arrangements for getting Joe back and forth to therapy. Denise offered to take Joe to therapy each morning because it was on her way to work. What a blessing. I worked each morning until noon and would pick him up later in the day. While we were still talking, Joe got up from the table and started walking toward the bathroom. He just got up out of the chair by himself and took off walking. Denise and I looked at each other, and we just raised our eyebrows and watched him closely. We could tell that he was trying to make decisions on his own, but we had to keep an eye on him and watch so he wouldn't fall. I made sure he was okay in the bathroom, and he walked back to the kitchen by himself. While we were talking, we were listening to Cajun music; Joe loves music so I asked him if he wanted to dance, and he nodded yes. We didn't move our feet, but we danced.

Whenever Joe didn't have to go to rehab, Barbie, his sister, came down to stay with him. One day, when I came in from work, she told me Joe said he wanted her to take him home. He was going to leave a note to let me know where he was. He wanted to go home because he missed our son, Brian, and wanted to see him. Our other son, Tony, was staying with us in Alton, so he did get to see him, but not Brian.

It was so cool, because right after I came in the door, Brian arrived for a visit; Joe was so happy to see him. He stayed and had pizza with us, which Joe wanted to try, so I scraped all the large food from it, and he tried some tiny pieces of crust. He said that he wanted a taste of 7-Up soda; he just rinsed his mouth out with it but didn't try to swallow any of it. He had a good time.

It was the end of May, and Joe's doctor wanted him to do therapy five days a week. She thought he was up to it. I would be going back to work full time and had to work out the details of getting Joe back and forth. I spoke to her about what to expect at the end of June, when he was done with therapy in St. Louis. She told me she didn't expect Joe to need physical or occupational therapy, but he would need speech therapy two to three times a week for up to six months. He should be able to do that closer to home, so hopefully, we'd be able to move home before long. She also said that Joe wouldn't need eye surgery. There was nothing wrong with his eyesight, but the muscles behind his eye were weak; the eye patch should strengthen the muscles, but it could take up to eight months. If it did not correct itself, he would need to see a neurologic ophthalmologist.

I needed help explaining to Joe why he still could not eat food. We were invited to a graduation party, and I knew I'd have to tell Joe he could not eat the food there; we would go to the party after the meal was over.

That did not work out because people were still eating when we got there, and Joe thought it was okay to eat too. I told him that he might not do so well, but he tried it anyway. He did choke on all of it and could not stop coughing; I felt so sorry for him, but he wanted to go so badly to see everyone. I was upset, and he got upset with me. We just should not have gone.

I spoke to Joe's doctor about his swallowing issue, and she said she would warn Joe about eating. I felt it was my fault because we went to the graduation party. She said that she'd be testing different foods later in the week. Her concern was that he could silently aspirate and then develop pneumonia and fever, and we sure did not want that.

A benefit auction had been planned for Joe in Carrolton, and there was also a pancake and sausage breakfast the same day; we went to the auction and saw so many family and friends. The auction lasted until late afternoon, so we decided to stay at our house that night. We were so overwhelmed by everything that had been done for us. The people in our hometown had surely stepped up to be there for our family. Truly a blessing.

I had trouble with the feeding tube that night and the next morning. I thought, *Wouldn't you know it?* I couldn't figure out why I had trouble because I had done it so many times. That night, I also noticed something was different about Joe's forehead. His scar looked different to me, so the next day, I took Joe to therapy because his doctor would be there.

When we saw her, I took off his Band-Aid, and we could see the metal plate in his forehead. It was like it just appeared. She said Joe would need to see a plastic surgeon. At first, she said he could wait until his intensive therapies were done, but then she suggested that I check with my insurance and have it done. I called Lisa and explained that I wanted to take Joe back to the doctor who did the original surgery. She said she would check to see if we could, since he was not on our insurance plan.

I also found out that the feeding tube entry was fine, and he no longer needed to take medication for his stomach; this was great news, and the tube could be removed within three weeks. He was scheduled to have a swallow test done next week, and if he passed, he would be able to have pureed foods (which we had been doing a little of, anyway). The nurse also taught me a technique for Joe's tongue with Italian ice and a long Q-tip. It did seem to help with his swallowing and saliva. The doctor also told me it was important for Joe to maintain his weight; it would not be good for him if he gained any. She filled out the paperwork, so it was all ready when he started speech therapy closer to home.

She wanted to check Joe's balance before we left, so she used the Romberg test, which assesses the body's sense of positioning. It is used to detect the cause of motor coordination loss; she had him stand up, feet together, and arms out straight in front of him with palms up and his eyes closed, and he did super. He did not even swerve. After checking his balance, she told us she wanted to stay on his case until he no longer needed her; if our insurance would not pay her, then she would not charge us. She asked if that was all right with us. Yes: another amazing blessing.

On June 11, Lisa, our insurance representative, called and told me she spoke to a neurosurgeon, who recommended we go back to see the neurosurgeon who did the original surgery. So she called Dr. Pencek's office and spoke to his nurse, who said it wasn't normal to see the metal plate in Joe's forehead; she went ahead and made the appointment. I was so happy because I wanted him to see Joe instead of someone else who would not know Joe's case.

You know, we were taking life one step at a time each day, not knowing what would happen next; other things kept happening too. I started receiving bills from the hospitals and doctors; for some reason, they had not been sent to the right insurance company. I'm not sure how that happened, but I spent many hours on the phone trying to fix it. I had a note on every statement that I received explaining how it had to be fixed. I received page after page of statements; one bill that we never did receive was for the helicopter when Joe was taken from Carrolton to Springfield. Many people asked if my insurance paid for that, and I always said, "I don't know because I never got a bill for the helicopter trip." Not one piece of paper. God was with us even in the very beginning. It was not easy to keep track of every bill that was sent to me, especially when you saw totals close to one million dollars. Around that same time, I found out that lightning must have hit our house and gone through the TV and VCR; I had to call our home insurance company to take care of that problem.

On June 12, you'd never guess what Joe did while we were at our house. Some friends came by to see us, and one of them, Eric, asked Joe to cut his hair. He had let his hair grow since Joe's accident and was not going to let anyone else cut it but Joe. While Joe was cutting his hair, there was a knock at our door; it was two people who had read about Joe in a newspaper and wanted to let us know they were selling products to help with a recovery fund for Joe. We knew nothing about that going on, but they were sure happy to meet Joe. It was another time when God worked in mysterious ways.

That same day, we received a phone call from a woman who had sent Joe a card in March; the card had a check in it, and she had not received the cancelled check back so she wanted to make sure that we received it. I went digging through all the cards (when we counted them later, there were over seven hundred). I couldn't believe it, but I found the card, and the check was inside. I thought we had looked at all the cards, but we somehow missed one. I took it to the bank so they could return it to the lady. I was so glad that I was able to find it for her.

On Sunday, we all went to church together for the first time since the accident. I wasn't sure how Joe would do for a long period of time, but he did good. Everyone was so happy to see him and me and the boys; Pastor Sam was extremely touched when he saw Joe.

It was a great day until we got back from church, when I noticed that Joe's leg was swollen. I took his shoes off, and his foot was purple and felt cold. I thought that maybe his leg was in the down position for too long, so I quickly elevated it with some pillows. Not long after that, he was sick to his stomach. I wasn't sure what was happening, but his body was telling me something. I started thinking it had something to do with the blood clot they had found in his leg.

I asked Joe if his leg hurt, and he said yes and that his left side was hurting. It came on quickly. We all laid hands on Joe and began to pray and pray hard. Joe had gone to church that day, and so many lives were touched; we were not going to let our guard down or try to figure things out for ourselves or become fearful. Joe's swallow test was going to be soon, and after he passed the test, he'd be able to eat and talk better, and then it would be testimony time. I kept checking on Joe's leg; it didn't get any worse, so we kept praying. Another attack on Joe's body.

Tony was so touched by God's power. Joe became so calm and peaceful, and he fell asleep. Tony was crying and said, "Mom, God is so good, isn't He? He is good, isn't He, Mom?"

Yes, Tony; God is good, all the time.

I needed to let Joe's doctor know what was happening, so I called her the next morning; she said he should see his primary care physician, so we made an appointment for that morning. Dr. Voigts told us that Joe had bronchitis, which we had not thought of because he had been coughing for a long, long time due to his inability to swallow correctly. He believed the pain in his left leg was caused by the blood clot, which was still in his leg. He gave Joe a shot of antibiotic and a prescription to take at home. He said Joe should be better in a couple of days.

The next day, Joe had an appointment with Dr. Pencek, the neurosurgeon. Joe did feel better and we needed him to check the scar on Joe's forehead. Denise's brother-in-law fixed up his Suburban so Joe could ride comfortably in the back. He put a mattress in the back and Joe could lay down and prop his leg up while traveling to Springfield; he slept all the way there. He was able to walk into the doctor's office, and when Dr. Pencek came into the room, he was amazed when Joe gave him a big handshake. The nurse asked Joe his name, his birthdate, and my name. Joe told her my real name, which is very unusual, and then said I had some explaining to do about my name. It was funny that Joe told her my real name instead of my nickname, which is what I use all the time.

Dr. Pencek looked at Joe's forehead and said the surgical area needed to be repaired; he hoped that could happen within the next couple of weeks. He said that the repair should be rather simple. He then checked Joe's eyes because he was wearing an eyepatch; he said that neurologically, he did not care for eye patches because some muscles get pulled too strong one way; we would deal with that issue another time.

Dr. Pencek then looked over at me and asked if I had seen Joe before the surgery; I told him that I had. He then began to tell me how bad the injury was. He said that the fracture was star shaped, and he pulled out lots of bone, hair, and pieces of wood. We discussed the multiple fractures, and he said that there were probably over one hundred; he told me it reminded him of a cracked eggshell. I couldn't help but cry. It brought back so many memories.

The doctor then took the pen he was holding, pointed toward Joe, and asked, "What is this?"

Joe looked over at me and smiled because he thought the doctor was pointing to me and that he should say my real name again.

I told Joe to tell the doctor what he was holding in his hand; I could tell by looking at Joe's face that he was wondering if the doctor thought he didn't know what a pen was. I couldn't help but giggle.

Dr. Pencek hadn't seen Joe since he was flat on his back and unable to move one single part of his body. He told me he thought there might be something neurologically wrong. He told us he would like to see Joe again, and even though the insurance wouldn't pay his bill, he would see him at no charge. He really wanted to keep up with Joe's progress. What a blessing. Praise the Lord.

When we were back home, Lisa called to let me know that Joe had an appointment next week with Dr. Rhinehart, a facial cranial plastic surgeon at St. Louis University. It really helped that she and Dr. Pencek were able to get the appointment made so quickly.

For supper that night, I pureed some ham, potatoes, and peaches and Joe did really well, but when I fed him through the feeding tube before bed, he got sick to his stomach. I wasn't sure why, but something good did happen at suppertime: Joe wanted to say the blessing before the meal. It brought tears to my eyes because it was the first time since the accident; Joe always loved saying prayers at mealtime.

I called Dr. Voigts office the next morning, and he put Joe on some medication for his stomach. I remembered that he had been on that medication previously but was taken off it; I would have Joe try it again to see if it helped this time. I was confused about his eating because sometimes it worked, but other times, not so well.

The medication was working for Joe this time. On June 18, he told me he wanted ham, eggs, and potatoes for breakfast, and to my surprise, he did fine. He wanted to try coffee, which he had always loved, so he drank some but sadly couldn't keep it down.

Denise told me that day that she would be glad to stay with Joe while I worked. I was so happy and so at peace, knowing that she would be with him. One day, she told me that she filled out paperwork for the Walmart Sam Walton fund; they offered five-hundred-dollar, one-thousand-dollar, five-thousand-dollar, and ten-thousand-dollar awards for community leadership. I had never heard of that fund, but it was wonderful that she did that for us.

Joe seemed different somehow now; I couldn't quite put my finger on why exactly, but he was a lot more alert and looked really good. I wanted to see how his leg was doing so I took the support hose off; to my surprise, his leg was close to normal size.

God was continuing to do a great work in Joe!

CHAPTER 14

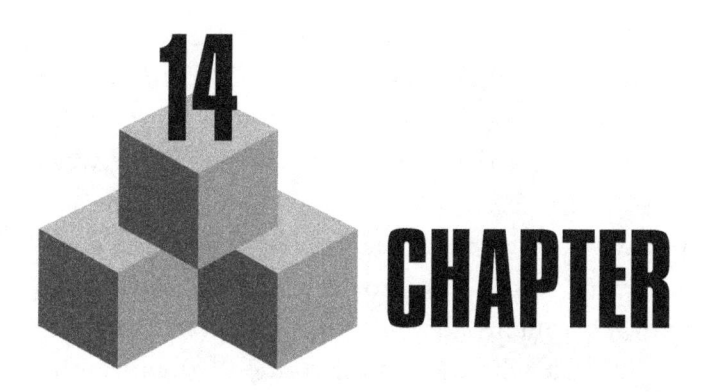

On June 21, we went to St. Louis University (SLU) Hospital to see the plastic surgeon. When I picked Joe up at two o'clock, the therapist told me he did good with the food that was given to him. She said, "Perfect, actually," and told me she had the idea that he'd been eating at home. Joe looked at her and asked where she got that idea. Hmmm. She was going to try liquids with him the next day.

We arrived at SLU about three o'clock, and they took Joe directly back to a room. Dr. Rhinehart told us the scar area was infected; he needed to see if there was a piece of bone or something else causing the infection; if a piece of bone was lodged in the plate, he could smooth out the area. The surgery was scheduled for the next week. Dr. Rhinehart could not get over how well Joe and I were both doing, and he asked me some questions to make sure that I was doing all right. It was so nice of him to be concerned about me too; he told me he knew I had been dealing with a lot of stress. He also suggested that Joe be seen by an ophthalmologist to check his eyes; they could possibly give him a see-through patch that could pull both eyes together at the same time. That would be amazing for Joe.

When we were back home, Barbie called to let me know she had suggested to Dr. Voigts that Joe's blood clots were connected to his respiratory issues. Each time Joe's leg had been swollen, he also had respiratory trouble. The doctor said they could be connected, and suggested Joe take an aspirin a day as a blood thinner. I really appreciated her sharing with me what Dr. Voigts had to say, but I couldn't start Joe on the aspirin until after the surgery on his forehead; I also wanted to learn more about the connection between the two conditions.

Joe needed to have a chest x-ray to see if the bronchitis was gone. I scheduled the x-ray, and on our way into the hospital, a lady stopped us and said she knew us from his story and was glad to see him doing so well. Then the woman who did his registration recognized his name and told him he was amazing. She said she believed that Joe survived the accident by the grace of God, and she told us she had been keeping up on his progress. It was so nice to hear that people were still following his story.

The next day, when I picked Joe up after therapy, I found out that he had gone to the vending machines and got himself a can of tea and a package of crunchy Cheetos. When the speech therapist saw him with the food, she quickly grabbed them out of his hands and threw it all away. I told her I didn't appreciate her grabbing them from Joe instead of explaining why he should not have them. I was upset with her actions, but she didn't seem concerned. This was not good. When she tried then to give him something to drink, he told her no. He asked her for a straw but could not have one, so he didn't drink anything for her. I knew I would have to keep an eye on this situation.

The chest x-rays were clear and showed that his fractured rib had healed perfectly. Praise the Lord.

Dr. Rhinehart also ordered new x-rays of Joe's forehead for him to be able to compare with the x-rays from the night of the accident.

June 27 was the evening of Joe's class reunion. He told me he wanted to go, so I asked his brother, Dick, if he'd help me get Joe there; of course, he was happy to help. We did not go for the meal but arrived later to visit. We didn't stay long, and while we were getting ready to go, I told him that his classmates wanted to see that "Joe Lakin smile."

He said, "They will because Joe Lakin is alright."

It made me want to cry. He enjoyed the evening so much, and they did a special toast in his honor. It was so nice.

His doctor ordered a new medication for him to take for the coughing. He was able to take the tablet by mouth, but about ten minutes later, he started coughing and couldn't quit; he was having a hard time breathing. It scared me, so I called Barbie, who told me to give him the medication through the feeding tube with some water; she also suggested putting a cold rag on his neck and lifting his arms above his head. It calmed him a little, but he was still coughing; he coughed the medication back up that I had given him. After a while, he fell asleep; I prayed and prayed, and I stayed awake all night to make sure he was all right. When he got up the next morning, he was fine, like nothing had ever happened. He said he was hungry and wanted some grits for breakfast. I was a little hesitant but thought that we could sure try, and he did fine with them.

I took him for his swallow test that day, so while he was having that done, I called Dr. Voigts to discuss what had happened the night before; he didn't think Joe had a reaction to the medication, and he prescribed some nasal spray to help with the nasal drainage. He suggested that Joe's feeding tube could have been pushing against the vasal vagal nerve in his stomach, and that could have affected his respiratory system. That was something I needed to investigate.

I received a call later in the day that he had failed the swallow test; we had to continue with pureed foods. That's really all I was told; I didn't get to ask any questions about it. I decided to call them later. It seemed like so much was happening all at once, but it had been like that for months.

I also received a call letting me know that the surgery for his forehead was scheduled for July 7.

On July 2, Joe was discharged from Hazelwood; that meant we could move back to our house, our home. Our new insurance didn't cover Hazelwood or Joe's doctor. I had to choose between Jerseyville Hospital Rehab or Alton Memorial Rehab.

Before I checked the facilities to see which would be best for Joe,

I asked him where he'd like to go, and he said, "I want to go home and stay there."

I knew he had to be tired and probably wondered why this had to keep going on and on and on.

When it came to Sunday, we all went to church and then moved our things out of Mark and Denise's. It was such a hard thing to do and very emotional for all of us. The daily walk that they have with God touched my life in such a special way. They did so much for all of us, and we could never repay them; it was something we will never forget, and we will love them forever.

The next day, we woke up in our own home. I admit that it felt strange. I did need to go to the store, and while I was there, a lady came up to me and gave me a big hug; she told me that she had been keeping up on everything that was happening with Joe, and then she added that people were saying that I had been a rock through all of this trial. I told her that it had definitely been hard, but it had all been for the glory of God, and He had given me so much strength that could only come from Him. She hugged me again with tears in her eyes and said she was so happy she had the opportunity to talk to me.

July 7 was the day of Joe's forehead surgery. It was supposed to start at 11:30 a.m., but they didn't take him back until 1:30. Before the surgery, they came in and took four vials of blood; he had antigens in his blood due to his previous blood transfusions, and there needed to be a match. The nurse had a hard time finding a good vein to put an IV into, but he had had so much done to him that I really wasn't surprised. A chest x-ray was also taken because of his bad cough.

The surgery was started at 3:15 p.m., and the doctor came out at five o'clock and told us he removed the infected area from the plate; he would reform it in three to six months. He also said he found a mesh-like material between the plate and his skull; he had never seen that material before, so he called Dr. Pencek during the surgery. He then called a neurosurgeon to come in and look at it. He also said he was aware of Joe's cough and thought it may be caused from cranial fluid drainage; he decided to check that out during another appointment. I wasn't sure if that had been the cause after all this time. The cranial fluid leakage had not been talked about for some time. Finally, he told us that the chest x-ray was clear, and his temperature was normal. There was no mass in his lungs from aspiration, and his esophagus looked fine too. Joe got back to his room at 7:30 p.m. It had been a long day, but it was all truly a miracle.

A week later, we went to see Dr. Rhinehart for a follow-up visit. He said that everything looked great and predicted he could go back in and reconstruct Joe's forehead in three months. He originally thought it would take six months, but his forehead was healing extremely well. He told me he wanted to continue to see Joe to make sure he received the care he needed. He said he didn't believe the feeding tube caused the coughing, but he was still concerned that it could be the cranial fluid drainage. He wanted Joe to see the neurosurgeon, who would be able to check on the fluid by injecting a dye to show if there was any leakage. He thought it could be a possibility because of the force that came down on Joe's head. We now have an appointment with the neurosurgeon.

Dr. Rhinehart then said that he agreed with Joe taking an aspirin a day for the blood clot, but not to start taking it yet because of his recent surgery. He said Joe didn't have to keep his forehead covered all the time, and he could now get the area wet. He also suggested that Joe take Robitussin DM for the cough. It was sure worth a try.

On our way home from the doctor appointment, Joe had his first therapy at Jerseyville Rehab. The therapists evaluated Joe and said they were very impressed with what he could do, considering how bad the injury was. All of Joe's paperwork and test results had been sent there, and the speech therapist told us he couldn't explain the failed swallow test. Considering Joe has been eating food, he didn't understand the result. We didn't either.

On July 26, Joe saw Dr. Sherril in St. Louis; the neurosurgeon that was called in on Joe's forehead surgery. He did not believe that cranial fluid drainage caused Joe's cough and said Joe would have been really sick, in a different way than he had been, if that were the case, and he would have been diagnosed with meningitis; he would have had severe headaches, and fluid would have been running out of his nose. He checked Joe's ears and said he was looking for possible fractures in the middle ear, considering the force that hit him. If that were the case, then there would be a large amount of fluid in his ears, which would cause his loss of hearing.

He felt like the coughing could be caused by throat mechanics not yet working properly. He said, "Please give it time because with a severe brain injury, the speech and swallowing would be affected and the last to come back to work correctly."

I asked him if I should take Joe to an ENT specialist, and he said not to consider doing that for at least a year. It could take that long for the throat mechanics to work again correctly, but they would. He told me that he and Dr. Rhinehart were happy to see that the infection in his forehead around the plate was only on the outside of his skull, instead of working from the inside to the outside. He said he only had to scrape a very small piece of the skull to get all the infection. He said he didn't think he needed to be present when reconstructive surgery was done in a few months.

Dr. Sherril was very informative and patient with us. A nurse came into Joe's room and asked about his injury. I explained how it happened, and she told me that her husband was going to trim the trees in their yard, but now she didn't want him to do it. I told her she should tell her husband that she met someone who was severely injured while trimming trees and to have a professional do it.

Later that evening, Tony was thrilled when it was bedtime because he gave Joe a hug good night, and Joe told him, "Drive careful." It was funny to us, but Tony knew that his dad used to tell him that when he would leave for work every morning. It showed us that more of Joe's personality was coming back.

It was therapy day again, and his physical therapist said that Joe could walk five minutes on the treadmill at home, as long as someone was nearby, and he no longer needed to bring his wheelchair with him to therapy because he didn't use it there. She said she would not be surprised to see him back in the salon cutting hair by the end of August and suggested three haircuts a day to start. I was totally surprised and thought that would not happen for at least a year.

His speech therapist gave him a Danish and a carton of milk, and he did great. She said she wasn't nervous at all while he ate, and he didn't cough or choke one time. We were so excited for him. She was going to call Dr. Voigts and recommend that the feeding tube be removed; she also noticed a considerable difference in his cough and speech in the last week.

She said, "Joe is defying all the odds."

We had heard that before and never tired of people saying it. I told her he had not been coughing much at night and was actually sleeping all night; it had been several months since he had slept all night. That was super exciting for Joe.

I was continuing to try to find an eye doctor. I was told to look for a doctor who specialized in the strabismus muscle. I wasn't having any luck so far finding a doctor that our insurance would cover, but I wasn't going to give up.

CHAPTER 15

On August 9, the feeding tube was removed. Joe's sister, Barbie, took him to the doctor because I had to work. She told me it bled quite a bit, and Joe said it hurt when it was pulled out. There was a compression bandage put over the opening, and it had to stay dry for twenty-four hours. He also checked Joe's leg because it was swollen and said to continue taking the aspirin for three more weeks; if the swelling did not go down, he would put him on a different medication.

Barbie said the doctor wanted to know how I was doing because he had not seen me for a while, and Joe told him, "Someone's gotta work."

Barbie called me later that evening and told me about the blood clot; she said Joe could have died from the clot the night it was found. She said the fact that he was already in bed at the hospital and the doctors were able to get the Greenfield filter in so quickly saved his life. I told her I believed that God raised his temperature that night to warn the doctors about the clot. God had been so faithful to us; I know I said this before, but God was definitely ordering every step.

I received a call the next morning from Lisa, the insurance representative who was so much help to us. We had sent her a gift along with an update on how Joe was doing. She told me saw a nurse who had taken care of Joe and told him about Joe, and he couldn't believe it. She also told Joe's case manager; she was so happy to hear the news and would be sure to tell Joe's doctor. They were all such a big part of why Joe was where he was now. With a lot of hard work and determination, they helped make his recovery possible.

In the middle of August, Joe wanted to go to the State Fair for the Township Official Day; we went, but I had to push him in a wheelchair. It was not easy to push him all over the place, but he had a fun time. While we were in Springfield, we decided to go to Memorial Hospital to see if anyone was working that would have taken care of him the month of March.

I first spotted Nola; she looked at me and then looked over at Joe and said, "Oh, wow, I can't believe I am looking at Joe Lakin. I have goose bumps all over my body."

She was shocked and took us over to the nurse's station, which I was very familiar with, and there stood; Tommy, Jan, and Jim. Jim saw us coming, and I heard him say, "Look who's walking down the hall." It was awesome to see all of them and especially awesome to see the shock on their faces. They were all a part of making sure that Joe stayed alive right after the accident.

The next day, I took Joe down to Boyd Hospital to see if the doctor who took care of Joe after the accident was there. He was, so I introduced them to each other; the doctor was, I'm not sure what word to put here, shocked, touched, and excited to see Joe up and walking. It was truly touching. The doctor told us the night of the accident that he wasn't sure Joe would make it, and Joe was now standing in front of him; he was the first doctor to see him after the tree limb hit his head. Truly amazing.

By the middle of September, Joe's occupational therapist told us he was on the high level of progress, which was surprising, considering his injury. His therapy was down to two times a week, and speech therapy only once a week. Next month, he would be going for a driving testing to see if he could drive. I hadn't even given a thought to Joe driving again.

We had another appointment with Dr Rhinehart; he thought Joe's forehead was healing nicely and wanted to schedule the reconstruction surgery for October. He told us we had three options to choose from:

1. Take some bone from another part of his body and place it in his frontal lobes.
2. Using a special CT scan to get a perfect computerized picture, fill the frontal lobes in with filler and metal.
3. Place filler in the concave area and replace the right frontal metal piece at the same time.

He wanted me and Joe to discuss the options and let him know so he could schedule the surgery. He also told me he recommended Joe not stay at home by himself, mostly because of his balance. He sure didn't want Joe to fall, especially since the reconstructive surgery has not been done. His forehead was an open wound. I had been considering having a health aide come to our house later than 7 a.m., but not anymore. I had to give more thought to this. I knew that Joe needed to start doing some things around the house. He needed to start feeling useful and to have a routine again, and I knew that was not going to be easy.

While we were in St. Louis, we went to SSM to see Joe's therapists; they were happy to see Joe and me. We also ran into Sheila, the hospital's representative who evaluated Joe at Memorial Hospital to see if he'd be accepted as a patient. She told us the doctors at Memorial were not very optimistic that Joe would ever amount to anything again.

She then said, "On paper, there is no medical way, but he truly is a miracle." She said she couldn't help but wonder herself.

Then we heard that Joe won a thousand-dollar award from Walmart, which would be presented to him at a township meeting. The head of the township heard about the honor and wanted pictures of him accepting the award to put in the township's magazine.

I was also asked to speak in front of a group of ladies, where I told the story of Joe's accident. I was nervous, but I did it. I did truly love sharing Joe's story and telling people how God would always be the God of our lives. No matter what.

September 26 was our anniversary. This anniversary was even more special because Joe was still here to celebrate with me. In the first few minutes after his head injury, I questioned whether we would have more time together, but look at us now.

Joe's birthday was October 14; I took the day off so Joe could see a psychologist for the Department of Social Security Disability; I need to tell you what a strange experience that was. Social Security told me to take Joe to a certain doctor, and it was not a good experience. The doctor worked out of his home, and it was cluttered and not professional at all. It made me nervous. The appointment lasted two hours; I felt like Joe would be denied disability, but we left it in God's hands.

On our way home, we stopped to see a doctor, who was not only our doctor before the accident but a friend. He admitted to us that he had not given Joe any hope. He said that after looking at him in the ICU after the accident and from speaking to Joe's nurses, he did not think he would make it, and if he did, he wouldn't be his old self.

October 19 was the day of Joe's forehead reconstruction surgery. We spent the night in St. Louis because he had to be at SLU at 6:30 a.m. We were taken to the Ambulatory Care Unit (ACU) area, and they ran many tests and asked lots of history questions. When the anesthesiologist came in, he asked Joe if he was anxious, and Joe said, "Yes." He gave Joe an injection to calm him down and said Joe was what they called nervous anxious. They came to take Joe for surgery at 8:15 a.m. and then called at 9:10 to say that the surgery had started.

I received a call at 11:40 a.m., when the surgery was finished. He was in recovery for an hour; I thought he was being taken back to the ACU area, but when we arrived, he wasn't there, so we went back to the surgical waiting area. A nurse came and said that Joe was having a hard time waking up; she said she'd let me know when he woke up. A lot of thoughts went through my mind; I wondered if something had happened because of the head injury or if it was too soon after the accident to do this reconstructive surgery. I don't think Dr. Rhinehart would have suggested the surgery if it had been too soon. About fifteen minutes later, I was told that he had been taken to the ACU area. He was not totally coherent yet, but the nurses said he would be able to go home later.

Dr. Rhinehart came out and said that the surgery went very well; the brain lining looked excellent. He made an incision across the top of his head from ear to ear but didn't have to shave any of his hair; the stitches were on the inside, and he used a new type of glue. Joe would need to keep his head propped up at 30 degrees for two weeks. He would also be taking Tylenol with codeine and an antibiotic during recovery.

Next, the anesthesiologist came in to tell us more about the surgery; two titanium plates were inserted into Joe's forehead; they were 6mm thick, like a sheet of aluminum foil (that's incredible when you think about it). I said I didn't feel good about taking Joe home that night because he seemed so out of it. He said he would speak to Dr. Rhinehart, and they agreed that Joe should stay at the hospital overnight. Once he got into a room, he said he was hungry, so I told a nurse; after a while, they brought him some Jell-O and broth; he ate the Jell-O, but after a short time he was sick to his stomach. We stayed with him until 8:30 p.m., when visiting hours ended. No one had been in to check on him since the food was brought to him, so I was definitely not comfortable leaving him at all.

The next morning, the boys and I got to the hospital at eight o'clock; when we got into Joe's room, he had not eaten yet, so I told the nurse he was ready for breakfast. He was brought some cold cereal, fruit, cranberry juice, and a cold muffin; it didn't seem like a good breakfast to me. He was so swollen that he couldn't see out of his left eye; he was starting to bruise badly, but the doctor had told us to expect the swelling and bruising. Then Joe told us that he kept punching the nurse's light last night because he had to go the bathroom, but no one ever came in, so he got up by himself and made it to the bathroom. Not good, considering the swelling and not being able to see out of one eye, and his balance was not so good. I was glad when he was released later that morning.

The next morning, Joe was really swollen and bruised; he slept most of the day. When he woke up, I asked him if his head was hurting, and he said, "No, not at all." Praise the Lord.

We went back to see Dr. Rhinehart for a follow-up visit on

October 25, and he was very pleased with how well Joe looked. He said that if we wanted, in about six months, he could repair the scars on his forehead; it wouldn't be considered cosmetic since it would still be part of the original injury. The plates over his forehead reminded me of a window screen. They wouldn't set off an airport scanner, and no one would ever know they were in Joe's head unless an x-ray was taken. He explained to us that Dr. Pencek had put odd pieces of metal on the left side of Joe's forehead because the fracture was oddly shaped; that was why he had to replace the entire forehead. He said Dr. Pencek had replaced part of Joe's brain lining, and he did an excellent job. I remember when Dr. Pencek came out during surgery and told us he needed God to direct his hands. So God did.

In December, Joe had his first driver's training; he passed with flying colors, but I was still hesitant about him driving. I knew it was hard for him not to be able to drive, but now I would worry about him out on the road, especially his decision-making ability.

One day, it hit me hard that I missed the old Joe so much. I tried not to think about it every day because it made me so sad. One evening, he called me his sweetie; it had been so long since I had heard him say those words to me. I wanted so bad to have my Joe back. I truly missed his love and compassion; he always had so much love for other people too. I always felt so special because he always treated me that way. Everyone knew how crazy we were about each other. I know that God isn't finished with Joe, so we will be okay.

I was glad when my sister, Susie, called me that day. She said she had been to see the doctor we used to go to, who had come to see Joe when he was in ICU. She said he told her that Joe was back to work in the salon, and she told him that he was driving now too. He told her that Joe was truly a miracle man; when he saw Joe in ICU and read the surgeon's notes, there was no way medically that Joe should have been alive. He said his body was going through a severe trauma, and that was why he told me I needed to be prepared.

He then told her about some people who lived in a desert area and had been without rain for a very, very long time; a group of them decided to pray for rain. Of course, many of those who came did not believe that prayer would work, but then he said that I would have brought an umbrella. Susie told him that I had never had a negative thought about Joe's recovery. He told her that was where my faith kicked in. I thought it was so exciting that the doctor shared all of this with her; it was my hope that Susie would fall even more in love with God.

On December 11, I received a call from a lady whose boyfriend was in Memorial Hospital. He had been in an automobile accident and was thrown from the vehicle. She said he had internal injuries and had to be brought back to life once. He was in a coma but not a sedated coma, and the doctor had told her that when he moved, it was his reflexes, and it would never be any more than that.

I talked to her for a long time and shared Bible scriptures with her that had helped me through tough places. I asked her if Jesus was her Savior and told her she should put her trust in Him and believe for the impossible to happen; even when everything looked bad, she could expect God to be there for them. I shared with her what Denise told me that I was able to gain strength from. She told me to look at Joe and say, "Even though he's not walking, talking, eating, or breathing on his own, I expect him to walk, talk, eat, and breathe on his own one day because of who God is." I expected God to move over him.

I told her that I would be praying for them and believing with her.

CHAPTER 16

By December 27, Joe was done with therapy; after the evaluation was done, they were surprised, especially because of his resistance strength. Joe was beginning to gain more weight, which was not a good thing, but it was hard to make him understand why it was not good. We would have to continue to work on that.

It was January now and a new year. We were asked if we'd be willing to speak during a Sunday school class with maybe a dozen people. We said, "Sure," but there ended up being two hundred people. They just kept coming in; it was wonderful. We couldn't get through the whole story because there were so many questions for us. We were convinced that this was what God had planned because we were able to speak to so many people. Unexpectedly.

The next day, we received a call wanting to know if we could tell Joe's story at the Illinois Businessmen's Fellowship meeting. We agreed to speak at their meeting, but it didn't go as well as before; they recorded our story, and one side of the tape turned out all right, but the other side did not. It was strange because you could hear what I was saying, but it wasn't my voice. Something very strange was going on; maybe Satan did not want me to get the story out there.

The next day, we drove to Springfield to see Dr. Pencek, the neurosurgeon who did Joe's surgery on March 1. He thought Joe's forehead looked great and asked us what Dr. Rhinehart placed inside his forehead. He was pleased that it was titanium. He looked at me and Joe and said, "I can't believe he is walking and talking." (Remember the prayer that I said when he was not walking or talking on his own?)

He then took Joe down the hall and introduced him to some of his colleagues. He told me they knew Joe's story, and he wanted them to meet him. He wanted to know what medications Joe was taking for the head injury; Joe and I at the same time answered, "None," and Dr. Pencek looked surprised. He just could not believe that Joe was standing there in front of him.

After we left there, we went to Memorial Hospital to see if some of Joe's nurses were still there; I especially wanted to see if Dr. Baker was there. One of the nurses paged him, and he called back to talk to me on the phone. He could not meet with us but had so many questions about everything. He gave me his work, home, and pager number. I hoped Joe would get to meet him someday. He told me that he knew Joe would beat all the odds. He told me he couldn't wait to share the news with some of his colleagues. He was truly thankful.

On January 24, Joe had an appointment with Dr. Rhinehart, who said that Joe's forehead looked great. He told us he would be glad to fix the scars if Joe wanted him to; Joe said, "The scars make my story more believable."

He said that Joe had a great sense of humor about all of it, but I knew he was serious. He said that the scar from ear to ear looked fine and just how he would expect it to look after three months. He wanted to see Joe again in the summer.

The woman whose boyfriend was in an automobile accident had called me and said that he had been transferred to St. Louis, so while we were down there, we went to the hospital to check on him. I was so excited to hear that they set a date for him to leave the hospital. I cried when I saw him because I knew that God had shown up for him too. Glory to God in the Highest!

The next time Joe and I spoke about his accident was February 14 at the Kane Baptist Church's Valentine's banquet, and it went very well. The pastor told us that he came to see Joe at St. John's after the accident. He said that so many people were upset about Joe's injury that he needed to go and see Joe for himself when he was in ICU.

He must have been there two days after the accident because when I asked him if I was there, he said, "No, I was told that you had stepped out for a minute."

He said that when he walked into the ICU area, they saw his collar and asked if they could help him. He told them he needed to see Joe and was told he could not speak to him because his inner cranial pressure was so high. He told them he just wanted to pray; they asked him if he was there to give Joe Last Rites, and he said, "No." He said he could tell that they didn't think Joe was going to make it.

March 1 came around again and it had been one year since the accident. I told Joe that I thought a lot of people would be thinking about him, and they were. He received a lot of phone calls, gifts, and cards, and he was even taken out for lunch. The whole day was an emotional roller coaster. So many thoughts and memories were going around in my head. Happy thoughts because Joe was doing so well, and sad ones when I relived those moments a year ago.

Joe continued to do well, but on November 22, I got up at 6:15 a.m. to get ready for work; I woke Joe around seven to make sure he was all right before I left. While he was in the shower, I fixed some breakfast. As I was walking to the bedroom, I heard a loud noise, so I looked around the doorway, and Joe was having a hard time breathing. I immediately thought that something was going wrong in his forehead with the titanium plate.

Just then, he fell on the floor and hit the back of his head on the pocket door on his way down. I was so scared; I called for the ambulance and yelled upstairs to Brian; he came flying down the stairs, and then I called Tony at work. Brian rolled Joe over on his side and laid his head in his lap; he kept talking to his dad. I could tell that Joe was not hearing him. I had no idea what was going on, but I couldn't believe we could lose him this time. I just didn't know what to do for him because I didn't know what was happening.

The ambulance arrived and took him to the hospital; they asked all kinds of questions to figure out what happened. They did blood tests, x-rays, and a CT scan. They wanted to compare the new CT scan with the ones taken in Springfield and St. Louis to see if this was caused by a new problem or the original head injury. When Tony got to the hospital, he found us praying in the chapel; he came over and gave me a big hug. He began to cry, and then we all began to cry. We had all been through so much.

The new CT showed no new cavity in the skull, which meant this seizure or convulsion was caused by the original head injury. I was told that Joe could have seizures all the time, but he never had one, or any headaches, either. When Joe hit the back of his head on the pocket door, the molding on the door sliced a piece of his scalp off, and he bled heavily. I thought immediately that he cracked his skull. Brian and I didn't know he was having a seizure. We had never been around anyone having a seizure. Joe also hurt the lumbar area of his back when he fell, because he hit so hard to the floor. He did get to go home later in the day and slept the rest of the day. What a whirlwind of a day, and once again, God showed up.

A couple of days later was Thanksgiving Day and Joe wanted to have dinner at our house, and we did. Everyone wanted to see Joe to make sure he was alright. He moved slowly that day, and his balance seemed to be more off than usual, but we made it through the holiday.

Our primary care physician called me the next day to ask how we were doing and talk about everything that happened. He suggested that Joe apply for disability, something we never ever considered doing. He said that with everything going on with Joe, we should consider it. He said he would do whatever he could to help us.

We also received a call from the hospital to see how Joe was doing. They told me to feel free to call anytime for anything, even if I just had a question or needed to talk. I appreciated knowing they were there for us.

Joe did not remember the day of the seizure at all. He did not remember getting up that morning, showering, or talking to me. He didn't remember going to the hospital or anything that happened there. He didn't remember coming home, not even the trip in the ambulance. He only knows what I told him.

Something still seemed to be going on with Joe's balance; there were times I had to hurry and grab him to keep him from falling. An MRI and an EEG were ordered, and we made an appointment with our doctor to discuss the results. The MRI showed that there was a short circuit on the left side behind the frontal lobe. I was told this would be a likely place for a problem because it was where the tree limb hit Joe. So being off balance could be expected.

It took a few days to get the insurance to okay the appointment, but on April 2, I was sitting in Dr. Zec's office while he did a neurophysiological assessment on Joe; he also talked to me for an hour and then gave me tons of paperwork to fill out. There was a personality scale, which covered things such as easily angered, shows poor judgement, is disorganized, talks out of turn, pays attention, and so on. There was also a cognitive checklist, which dealt with things such as difficulty remembering, activities of daily living, safety, routines, time, planning, and personal. I also had to rate his memory functions, executive functions, personality, attention, and concentration. There was so much more to rate Joe on; it felt like I was taking a test myself. I guess I was, sort of.

It seemed to take forever to answer the questions, but Joe was in the evaluation for eight hours. The doctor recommended that I write in a journal and assess Joe's day, using a number or letter system, such as 1 for a good day and 5 for a bad day, or A for a good day and D for a bad day. I made a list of what he could and could not do each day and kept him busy so he would not move into a vegetative state. He said there was one important thing to remember: There was nothing Joe could do about this. He said that the sparks that once were set off in the brain just were not being set off now. He said some things would change, and many would never come back.

I had several hours to sit and think about things. You know, sometimes life just goes on, day after day, same old thing; nothing different really happens. Then one day, after a split-second, everything changes. There were times Joe and I would talk, and we couldn't imagine why God would choose us to be together. We were so different, but God knows everything, including who we are and who we need in our lives. I was sitting there thinking about how God knew we would need each other, especially for such a time as this. Joe was always so strong and able to do anything he set his mind to, and now I had to be the strong one to help him. Only God knew.

Later that evening, our friend Eric called; he wanted to let us know how much he cares about us and missed his best friend, Joe. He said he had been amazed at how God had touched so many people with Joe's accident and recovery. He told me he prayed all the time for me too, and if he had a choice, he would rather live through what Joe went through than what I went through every day. He said he knew my life would never be the same; he truly admired me, and not many women would stay in the place where I am. I had tears in my eyes as he spoke, and I told him that when Joe and I married, I said our vows before God, and I took them seriously. I told him I didn't feel like I was doing anything special but just what I wanted and needed to do. Eric and his wife were such a blessing to Joe and me.

On April 16, Joe had an appointment with Dr. Zec for more neuro testing. He was in testing for more than four hours and was tested in math, fractions, algebra (he told the doctor that he couldn't do algebra when he was in school, so he wouldn't be able to do it then), reading comprehension, and pronunciation of words. He was also given different situations and had to tell the doctor what he would choose to do. We had to wait for the results to come in the mail.

CHAPTER 17

When I got home from work on April 30, Joe was sitting in his recliner and told me that his lower back was hurting, and his legs were hurting too, especially the right one. He said he had to sit down twice while walking to his mom's house, which wasn't that far. I felt his legs, and the right one was swollen and tight and warm. I had a feeling something was going on with his blood clot. I called Barbie, and she came over and then told me to call Dr. Voigts, so I did. He had previously told me to call him anytime, day or night. I called him at home, but he wasn't there, but his wife gave me another number to call, and he picked up the phone. After I explained what was happening, he told me to get Joe to the hospital in Jerseyville, and he'd meet us there. So..., I did.

Joe was checked in, and I was told he had thrombosis in the right leg; his leg was double the size it should be. They put him on heparin and drew blood for the lab. We were told Joe would be taken by ambulance to Springfield Memorial, so Tony and I left the hospital at 9:15 p.m., and Joe was to leave shortly after that. We went home and got some things together, and then Brian and I left for Springfield. We got to the hospital around 10:45, but Joe wasn't there yet, which was surprising, since the ambulance had its lights and sirens on.

He was brought in around 11:30 p.m., and we learned that the ambulance had been involved in an accident. A van ran right into it and spun it around several times. Everyone inside was alright but the ambulance could barely be driven. Joe had been strapped in, but the nurse was thrown around the inside. She told Joe she was glad he was okay, but she was done making any more trips like that.

The doctor came in and was very concerned because of the size of the clot. It went from his knee up to his groin area to the filter and was close to an inch in diameter. I had tears in my eyes as he spoke to me; I wondered what else Joe's body would have to deal with. He said they needed to make sure there was continued circulation to his toes, so they admitted him and continued the heparin. Joe was put into a room on the same floor that he was on after the brain surgery, which brought all kinds of memories back, but I was glad that he was at Memorial Hospital. I was surprised when the State Police Academy chaplain and a radio announcer from station WTSG came in to pray for Joe. That was so wonderful and just what we needed.

I decided to get a room at the motel next to the hospital for the night, but I only slept a few hours and was back to his room early the next morning. Dr. Solis wanted to continue the heparin to try to release the clot. Joe said that his leg and back were so sore that he could hardly move. When his nurse walked in, I recognized her; it was Jan, one of Joe's nurses two years ago. She said that Dr. Baker found out about Joe being here and would try to make it over to see us.

I also found out that the insurance company would not cover surgery at Memorial but would cover treatment in St. Louis. That made me so sad; I didn't want to take Joe there, so after several phone calls it was decided because of the size of the blood clot and the head injury earlier that they would cover the surgery for the clot. God is so good to us. Dr. Solis came in to give us three options. One was surgery, which involved making a very large incision and removing the clot. Two, catherization with a powerful clot buster medication, and three, continue medication at home until the clot dissolved, which could take up to a year. None of these sounded great to me; I was told that the first two options were very risky and could cause excessive bleeding.

Dr. Solis explained that he put the catheter in through the back of the leg and up through what he called an "enormous, humongous clot." He could not get all the way up through the clot to the filter, so instead, he came down through the top to get the clot buster medication in there and break apart the clot. They wanted the clot buster to dissolve the clot at the top. It could not be suctioned out until it dissolved. The catheter was left in overnight; he couldn't move his leg at all, and the doctor would go back in the next morning to suction the clot out. A restraint was put on his ankle, so his leg didn't move.

Joe was put in ICU overnight so he could be watched very closely. I was told that the catheter would drain overnight, and if there was any bleeding, they would have to call Dr. Solis. Joe told them he did not want to be sedated, and I didn't blame him because he had been sedated so much. His doctor came in and checked his leg; one of the residents asked if anyone had taken a picture of Joe's leg because he wanted to use it for his teaching. A cardiovascular doctor came in to look at Joe's leg too. He had heard about it and wanted to see for himself.

The next day, Joe went back in for the leg surgery; I was concerned because he said his leg was in a lot of pain. He did have a shot of pain medication at 4:30 and 8:30 a.m., and they came to get him at 10 a.m. His doctor came out at 11:30 a.m.; it did not go as well as expected. The clot buster had not dissolved any of the clot at the top or down by his knee, either. They were able to get some residue out of the middle above the knee to the groin. There was a large hematoma at the entrance site so they had to stop the clot buster medication because it could have caused excessive bleeding.

They told me that Joe would have to wear a compression hose on that leg from now on and would have to be on blood thinner. Dr. Solis hoped that Joe's body would break the clot up on its own, but it could take up to a year.

On May 5, I got to the hospital a little after 8 a.m.; Joe told me he did not sleep well last night, and his nurse said he had tried to go to the bathroom by himself. He was just starting to unhook himself from everything when she walked in. He told her he couldn't use the bed pan, so he had to get up. She went and got him a commode, which would have been a good idea all along. She told us that Joe would be moved back to the fourth floor that day.

Dr. Solis's assistant came in and explained that it was too risky to remove the remaining clot. It was not common to have a clot to be in a vein; it was more common in arteries; veins had valves to keep the blood going in one direction. Blood goes downhill with gravity in the arteries when the heart is pumping it, and it moves against gravity in the veins, so it can be dangerous to try a surgical procedure on the veins. There was a lot that could be affected.

Around ten o'clock, Dr. Baker walked into Joe's room; I was so happy to see him. I was excited to introduce Joe to him. He stayed about forty-five minutes and said Joe looked really good; he last saw him two years ago. He told me that back then, he had bosses telling him that Joe was not going to make it; they gave him a 5 percent chance to survive. He told me he knew with me as Joe's support system and my faith in God that he would defy all the odds and make it. It warmed my heart to hear how much we touched him. We always had such memorable long talks.

Joe was finally moved to a room at 8:15 p.m. The day had been extremely long.

Dr. Solis's assistant came in the next morning and said that Joe's leg should be elevated; it should have been elevated yesterday, but it was not. Joe's nurse came in and was unsure about giving Joe his blood thinner. He said Joe was on a massive therapeutic dose, and if he was supposed to get up and walk, then he shouldn't have another dose. The nurse went to get the doctor, who ordered another injection of heparin. He also said that the bandages would be taken off Joe's leg tomorrow. I told him I'd like for Joe to walk before he went home, and he said that was a good idea because more times than not, the patient's knees would be very weak.

On May 7, the bandage was taken off the back of Joe's leg; the doctor said that he could get up and walk a couple of times a day, with a nurse's assistance. He also said Joe should not do anything for two weeks and should keep his leg elevated as much as possible. He wanted Joe to use a heat pad on the back of his leg, which would help because the hematoma was soft, which was a good sign. I then asked the doctor how the blood was getting through the leg. He said the blood reroutes itself through the veins that are around the clot and crosses over the pelvis through the other veins. It's just how the body takes care of itself. He said he didn't want me to get alarmed when his foot and leg swelled, because they were going to do that for a while.

We waited since around 8:30 a.m. for Joe to be taken for a walk. Someone came in after lunch to measure his leg for a stocking he would wear when he walked, but he never got the stocking (we were told he would have it within the hour). His nurse came in to see if he was ready to go for a walk, which he wasn't because he didn't have the stocking; she said that the order for his walk must have been lost in the paperwork. She called the resident surgeon to see if Joe could walk with just an ace bandage on his leg, and he said, "Definitely not." He could, however, walk with a Tet hose and an ace bandage. She got him ready for his walk about 7:30 p.m. and said someone would be there in ten minutes. They came an hour later, and Joe went for his walk.

I got to Joe's room early the next morning because I didn't want to miss his doctor. I wanted to let him know what happened yesterday. He was very interested in what had happened and said he'd find out why Joe still didn't have his walking stocking.

When Joe's nurse came in, I told her that his pajamas needed to be changed; they hadn't been changed for three days. She brought some clean ones in for him. While she was still there, I told her the pillow and pillowcase under his leg also needed to be changed; they hadn't been changed since the surgery, and there was dried blood on it so she changed that too. I didn't really mean to be difficult, but these things happened, and they made me not want to leave him alone.

Dr. Solis came back in and explained that Joe would have to wear a compression stocking on his leg most of the time, not only when his leg was elevated, but most of the time. He said he wanted to see Joe in a couple of weeks, and there would be no charge for the office visit. He would not charge Joe for any of his treatment. What a blessing.

Joe was released at 4:15 p.m., and we got back home about 5:30; it was so good to be home. Barbie called and said she'd be glad to come over and give Joe the injection of heparin he needed every day. I told her it was important for Joe to walk each day, and she offered to help with that too. Sometimes, it took two people to help him walk, and I knew it was important to keep him moving as much as we could, but it wasn't always easy.

On May 21, Joe had an appointment with Dr. Solis, who was pleased at how well Joe was doing; he did not expect the swelling to be down so far. There was a small knot behind Joe's knee where the incision was made, but that was expected. He wanted Joe to keep walking as much as possible and as far as he could; he said Joe would know his limit. He was a little stumped by the soreness on the top of Joe's lower leg. He said he would have expected the upper leg to be sore but not the lower leg, so he wanted to see Joe again in two months and would do another doppler ultrasound then.

We had not been home for long when Dr. Voigts called me. He wanted to talk to me about how Joe was doing but also about the idea of Joe driving. He wanted to know how I felt about it. He was concerned that Joe could be distracted easily and might make the wrong decisions. He wanted to speak to Joe and me at his office sometime soon, but the thought of Joe driving made me very nervous.

There were times through all this when I needed to remind myself to continue to trust God and not try to lean on my own understanding. He had always taken care of us; there was still so much I didn't understand, but I kept praying that God would open new doors for us. I never dreamed this would be a part of our lives; well, not a part of it but all of it, but this was where we were now. Whenever I thought about this, I would remember what Denise told me: She said I shouldn't forget who I was and what I was; I should keep my eyes off the mountain and on the mountain mover. She also told me to call things that are not as though they were; that is where my faith and hope live. She said she did not want me to stop believing and to remember to always give it to God. So once again, I needed to dig deep down into myself and bring my faith and hope back where it belonged.

I made an appointment to see Dr. Voigts to discuss whether Joe should be driving; he was concerned about his impulsive control. Joe should have someone with him whenever he drives, for the first two months, anyway. It was really hard to have this discussion about Joe driving. So much had been taken away from him because of the head injury. It was not always easy to find someone who could take Joe whenever he wanted to go somewhere, but we would work it out.

One of the changes that was so different and difficult was that he would sometimes use foul language. That was unusual for us to hear. Joe never used language like that before. We were told that it came from the part of the brain that was affected by the injury. I was hoping it would not happen again but it would sneak up sometimes. Now, whenever we mentioned using foul language, he didn't remember saying that. That made it even harder to deal with, but it was another thing we have to work on.

Joe and I were asked to speak at the Street Invasion event on June 23. It went well, but we only had twenty minutes; that was not long enough to tell his story, but we did what we could. As we finished, Joe told everyone that they could call on him because he was back to stay. Our picture was in the town paper, and we never thought that would happen.

On July 23, we went to Springfield for another doppler scan on Joe's legs and to check for other blood clots. The doppler showed chronic blockage in the thigh area and upward. Dr. Solis said it must have been an old clot, and that was why he couldn't get through when he did the catherization. He said the body had taken care of it itself and rerouted the blood flow; there was every reason to expect the leg to give him trouble with the chronic blockage, but he was not in any pain.

I did ask Dr. Solis if Joe's filter was still working, and he said Joe was doing fantastic, considering what the doppler showed. If the filter was clogged, then Joe's legs would have both been swollen and sore, and he definitely would know it. The filter was put in the vena cava, where the two main veins come up from the legs; there must have been blood flow through the filter too, which was also amazing. Joe had once again been given a miracle.

CHAPTER 18

I realized more and more how all of this has changed Joe; he had lost control of everything he had before, and that must have felt strange to him. He had lost control of his life as he knew it, but God had a plan for him.

One day, while I was out walking, I realized that God had a plan, and I asked Him to draw me closer and show me something, so I could know He was still with us in this trial. I just needed to go for a walk and talk to Him. I also sent special prayers for Tony and Brian and for new jobs for them and for the godly women the Lord had already chosen for them. Later that morning, I received a call from Denise; she had been fasting and praying for all of us over the weekend. She told me she had asked God for a sign as she prayed and worshipped. She said she had sent prayers up for Tony and Brian and for new jobs for them and for the godly women God had already chosen for them.

We had been praying for the exact same things, almost word for word. I could not ask for a better sign from God than that.

Joe and I had a really good weekend; he seemed different somehow, and we did things together and went places together. It was so nice and an answer to prayer, for sure.

That October, a friend of ours, Roy, came to our back door and handed me two hundred dollars. I, of course, was shocked, but he told me it was our portion of the sale of the columns that we gave to him from our front porch. He sold them and wanted to give us a portion of what they sold for. I told him he didn't have to do that, but he insisted on us having the money. I gave him a big hug. Once again, God moved.

That same week, Joe got a different truck, not a new truck but a newer one. The cost was less than what we thought we'd be paying, so there was money left over. Once again, God moved.

Many thoughts and prayers prefaced our next big decision. After further discussion with our primary care physician, we decided to consult an attorney specializing in Social Security benefits to help apply for disability benefits. I took a large tub full of doctor's notes and test results to the lawyer; he couldn't believe how much there was. Several meetings were necessary to provide all the required information because so much had taken place that brought us to this point in our lives, following Joe's severe head injury.

On October 21, I opened an envelope from the Social Security Office of Hearings and Appeals, signed by a judge; the form said that Joe would be receiving a disability check each month. The first page was headed "notice of decision: fully favorable." I read through all the papers and the final paper stated the decision by the judge: full disability and disability insurance, retroactive to March 1, 1999, the date of the accident. It could have taken several months for a hearing, but it only took one month. We were never notified of a hearing date, so we didn't know when it was. I called the lawyer the next day, and he said there was no hearing; the papers went to the judge, and he signed it off as full disability. There were no questions asked. It really should have taken a whole lot longer. Once again, God moved.

The word *disability* was hard to accept, though. The judge had stated that there were definitely restrictions where Joe was concerned, and there was so much he could not do. He was now labeled disabled. It was hard to think of Joe being disabled and having restrictions; there was a time when he could do anything. Disabled is a place where he never wanted to be, but Joe's comment was, "Now I can contribute to the family." That was always most important to him: providing for his family.

I started saying the Jabez prayer every day that summer. This was the prayer:

> Oh, that You would bless me indeed and enlarge my territory
> That Your hand would be with me
> And that You would keep me from evil
> That I may not cause pain.

The Bible states that Jabez was an obscure man, more honorable than his brothers; his name meant "Because I bore him in pain."

In 1 Chronicles 4:10, Jabez was asking God to bless him greatly, exceedingly, abundantly. He was leaving it up to God as to how He would bless him. This was the only time that Jabez was mentioned in the entire Bible.

Since I started saying this prayer every day, siding was put on our house because of a blessing given to us, we were given two hundred dollars, we sold Joe's old truck and got a different one for less money and had money left over, and disability was accepted sooner than we thought it would.

There was one thing that Joe always seemed sure of, though. Whenever he told someone about his head injury and surgery, he always said that the doctor came out of surgery and told the boys and I that he wasn't going to make it, and we needed to tell him goodbye. Joe would say that my comment to the surgeon was, "Joe is going to be fine because we believe the report of the Lord." The Bible says, "Whose report will you believe? We shall believe the report of the Lord."

His report says I am healed; His report says I am filled.

His report says I am free; His report says victory.

Joe and I talked many times about what he believed he heard during the brain surgery. I always tell him that wasn't what happened, but the surgeon did come out and tell us several times that Joe was very critical and that he was doing everything he could.

The last time we talked about this, I heard a voice say to me,

"That is what Joe heard." I quietly asked myself, *That's what Joe heard?* I knew then that God was telling me that that is exactly what Joe heard during surgery, that he was not going to make it, and the boys and I would be telling him goodbye, but in Joe's spirit, he knew what my reply would be, and that was that he would make it.

I never really thought that Joe heard the surgeon say those words to us. God had not revealed anything like that to me before. I never could figure out why Joe kept telling his story like that, but now I know. Those words are what Joe really heard the surgeon say during his surgery, and it had been so real to him.

I am not writing this to tell you that everything is perfect, but is it okay? Sure. God is still in control of our lives and always will be. We have all been affected by Joe's accident. The boys continue to love the Lord will all their heart, soul, and mind. Tony lives in the same small town and has a great job. He is single and believes in God every day of his life. Brian is married to a lovely godly lady; they have two wonderful children (our amazing grandchildren), and he has a great job.

Every day is a challenge, each in its own way. Sometimes, Joe would tell me that I was the one who changed after the accident and he had not. I am sure that I changed; how could I not? But his was a drastic change, and the sad thing is that he did not know it. Joe still does not remember anything about the accident or everything he had to go through, except what I've told him; he does know more after reading this book. If you were to ask him if he was in any pain, he would tell you no because if he was, he didn't know it.

I praise God that He is continuing to reveal Himself to us about Joe's head injury accident, even today.

I am still working at the dental school and have been there more than twenty years. I continue to know without a doubt that God placed me there.

Joe and I still live in the same home we did when his head injury occurred; there are times when I walk through the house and cannot help being reminded of so many blessings from God; through all of our trials, many lives were touched and blessed.

Joe is doing great. He doesn't work but can completely take care of himself and is able to stay alone. He does things around the house, mows the yard, can still drive, and does whatever he wants. His long-term memory is amazing; he remembers things from a long time ago, and I say, "I can't even remember that." Sometimes, his short-term memory is not so good, but that's alright; that's an area of his brain that was affected.

Joe and I look forward to each day and wonder what God has in store for us to do; we know that God is ordering every step we take. This is the story of our compounded faith. I pray that your faith will also be compounded as you hold onto God's promises.

I want to leave you with these words: We all have a story to tell, and if we don't tell it, the story will end, and no one will never know.

Acts 20:24 says, "However, I consider my life worth nothing to me, if only I may finish the race and complete the task the Lord Jesus has given me, the task of testifying to the gospel of God's grace."

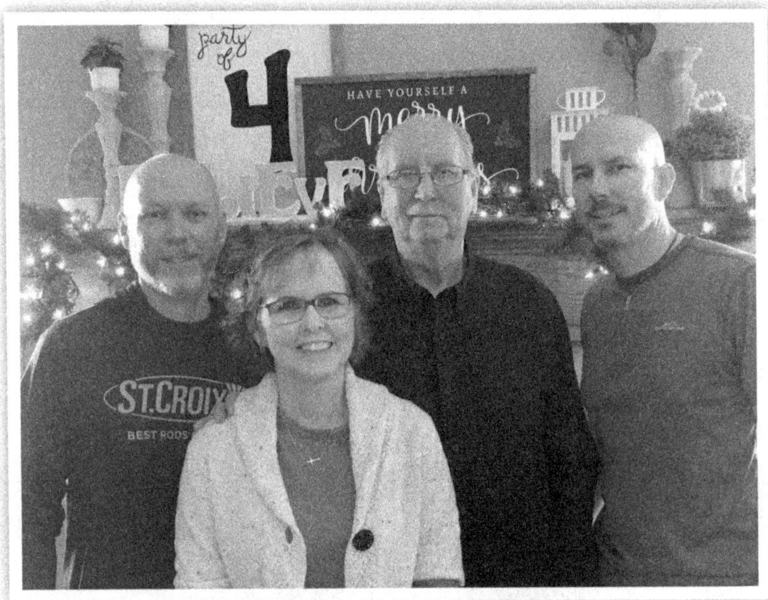
party of
4
HAVE YOURSELF A
ST.CROIX
BEST RODS

CPSIA information can be obtained
at www.ICGtesting.com
Printed in the USA
LVHW090819130221
679234LV00002B/2

9 781664 219625